The Memory Politics of the Cursed Soldiers in Poland

This book analyses right-wing memory politics in Poland through the concept of "cursed soldiers" as a key memory symbol, and how it has been used to construct a narrow and exclusionary vision of Polish identity framed in terms of Catholicism, national culture, and traditional family values.

Groundbreaking in its approach and combining top-down study with reception analysis, the book builds on the theory of hegemony, adding emotional dimensions to the understanding of memory politics and nationalism. It provides a detailed case study of Polish memory politics since 2015, when the Law and Justice Party (PiS) came to power, and offers insights into how historical memory is used to mobilise support within nationalist and populist movements. Through a range of data including interviews, participant observation, and analysis of various media, it presents a semiotic and emotional map of how these memory symbols are received and experienced in Polish society. The focus on Podlasie, a region with significant Belarusian population and a history of post-war partisan conflicts, highlights the complex interplay of memory, identity, and politics in contemporary Poland.

This work is intended for a broad audience, including undergraduates, postgraduates, scholars, and non-specialist readers such as booksellers or librarians.

Krzysztof Jaskułowski is Professor of Sociology at SWPS University in Warsaw. His research interests include nationalism, popular culture, and migrations. He is the author of *The Everyday Politics of Migration Crisis in Poland* and co-author of *Teaching History, Celebrating Nationalism: School History Education in Poland*.

Piotr Majewski is Associate Professor at SWPS University. His research interests include popular culture and nationalism. He is the author of *Rap w służbie narodu* [*Rap in the service of the nation*] and co-author of *Teaching History, Celebrating Nationalism: School History Education in Poland*.

Routledge Focus on the History of Conflict

The history of war and warfare often contains events and episodes that in themselves took place over a relatively short period of time but which have developed wider historical resonance. This series of books, part of the Routledge Focus series of short form volumes, usually somewhere between the average length of a journal article and a monograph, sheds a light on key topics within the history of conflict - taking a broadly international perspective and with all eras represented.

1 **German Anti-Nazi Espionage in the Second World War**
  The OSS and the Men of the TOOL Missions
  Jonathan S. Gould

2 **The Memory Politics of the Cursed Soldiers in Poland**
  Authoritarian Nationalism, Hegemony and Emotions
  Krzysztof Jaskułowski and Piotr Majewski

The Memory Politics of the Cursed Soldiers in Poland
Authoritarian Nationalism, Hegemony and Emotions

Krzysztof Jaskułowski and
Piotr Majewski

LONDON AND NEW YORK

First published 2024
by Routledge
4 Park Square, Milton Park, Abingdon, Oxon OX14 4RN

and by Routledge
605 Third Avenue, New York, NY 10158

Routledge is an imprint of the Taylor & Francis Group, an informa business

© 2024 Krzysztof Jaskułowski and Piotr Majewski

The right of Krzysztof Jaskułowski and Piotr Majewski to be identified as authors of this work has been asserted in accordance with sections 77 and 78 of the Copyright, Designs and Patents Act 1988.

The Open Access version of this book, available at www.taylorfrancis.com, has been made available under a Creative Commons Attribution-Non Commercial-No Derivatives (CC-BY-NC-ND) 4.0 license.

This work was supported by the National Science Centre. Grant Number: UMO 2019/33/B/HS6/00124.

Trademark notice: Product or corporate names may be trademarks or registered trademarks, and are used only for identification and explanation without intent to infringe.

British Library Cataloguing-in-Publication Data
A catalogue record for this book is available from the British Library

ISBN: 978-1-032-43785-9 (hbk)
ISBN: 978-1-032-43786-6 (pbk)
ISBN: 978-1-003-36884-7 (ebk)

DOI: 10.4324/9781003368847

Typeset in Times New Roman
by codeMantra

Contents

Acknowledgements   vii

1 Introduction   1

2 Nationalism, Hegemony, and Memory Politics   9

3 From Bandits to 'Cursed Soldiers'   20

4 Building Hegemony: The Memory Politics
   of Cursed Soldiers   32

5 Heroes? Partisans? Bandits? The 'Cursed Soldiers'
   from Below   67

6 Between Radicalisation and Contestation   105

   Index   109

Acknowledgements

This work was supported by the National Science Centre. Grant Number: UMO 2019/33/B/HS6/00124.

1 Introduction

Aim

The book analyses the right-wing memory politics in Poland through the prism of the concept of hegemony. We build on the theory of hegemony by introducing the notion of a key memory symbol that structures hegemonic memory projects. We go beyond a purely semiotic understanding of hegemony by supplementing it with an emotional dimension in the context of both the production and reception of the dominant memory project. The theoretical framework provides the tools for the empirical aim of the book, which is a case study of memory politics centred on 'cursed soldiers' (żołnierze wyklęci). We focus primarily on the Law and Justice Party (Prawo i Sprawiedliwość, PiS) after 2015 when the party won the elections and formed the government. Strictly speaking, PiS did not form governments on its own, but with the support of two minor parties. However, due to the dominance of the former party and for practical reasons, we will simply write about PiS governments.

Our starting point is an analysis of the national ideology of PiS, which we interpret as an exclusionary and authoritarian nationalism constituting an ideological response to the structural and cultural transformations of Polish society. PiS constructs such processes as the decline of Catholicism, non-European migration, and women's struggle for reproductive rights not so much in terms of social change but in the moralistic language of the decline of the Polish nation. It defines Polishness narrowly in terms of Catholicism, a 'thick' understanding of national culture and the so-called 'traditional family'. A narrow understanding of national identity translates into an authoritarian memory politics based on a retropian vision of Polishness as a patriarchal ethnocommunity.

We analyse the role of the past in the right-wing project of remodelling Polishness, focusing on the main element of PiS's memory politics, namely the commemoration of the Polish post-war underground (Polskie Powojenne Podziemie, PPP). We examine how and why the right wing invented the tradition of 'the cursed soldiers', transforming the PPP into an emotionally and ideologically charged symbol of resentment towards the system established after 1989 (Hobsbawm & Ranger, 1983). We explain why and how PiS took over and developed the symbolism of 'the cursed soldiers', elevating it to the status of a key memorial symbol in its antagonistic memory project (Bull & Hansen, 2016). We refer to this memory politics as hegemonic, but it is a hegemony by intention and not by its functions (Szacki, 1991). This process is still in progress and its success is not yet assured. We analyse the meanings, values, and emotions that the right-wing memory politics ascribes to 'the cursed soldiers'. The hegemonic discourse uses the term 'Cursed Soldiers', but we deliberately write 'the cursed soldiers' and use inverted commas and lower-case letters, which serves a distancing function. We see no reason why we should reproduce the official nomenclature, which is not so much descriptive as it performs persuasive-ideological functions. This does not mean that we claim objectivity (whatever that means) per se, but that we merely want to problematise ideological schemas.

We augment the top-down study of memory politics with an analysis of the reception of this politics, a kind of semiotic and emotional map of the readings and experiences of this symbolism in Polish society. We are primarily interested in what meanings and emotions the informants associate with 'the cursed soldiers'. Referring to critical media theory, we explore how top-down generated meanings and emotions are reproduced, negotiated, contested, and experienced in everyday life. Our analyses focus on the semiotic and emotional aspects of the reception of the symbolism of the 'cursed soldiers', paying less attention to memory activism. We do not attempt to present the full mnemonic landscape of contemporary Poland, but rather zoom in on the process of the assigning and reception of meanings and the emotional experience of this commemoration. An important context for our analysis is set by Podlasie, i.e. the north-eastern part of Poland inhabited in large part by the Belarusian population. Podlasie was one of the main areas of post-war partisans who not only fought against the communist authorities but also entered into conflicts with the local population, whom they accused of having pro-communist sympathies. The partisans exploited the local population, and some partisan units carried out ethnic cleansing among the Belarusian population, in whose communicative memory the traumatic experiences are still recounted today.

Rationale

Commemoration of the PPP occupies a central place in right-wing memory politics. For example, during the PiS government, two new museums were opened, i.e. the Museum of Cursed Soldiers and Political Prisoners of the Polish People's Republic in Warsaw (Muzeum Żołnierzy Wyklętych i Więźniów Politycznych PRL), and the Museum of Cursed Soldiers in Ostrołęka (Muzeum Żołnierzy Wyklętych). The right-wing government also introduced reforms in education, including history education, placing greater emphasis on learning about the PPP (Jaskulowski & Majewski, 2023; Jaskulowski et al., 2022). Successive presidents of the Institute of National Remembrance (Instytut Pamięci Narodowej, IPN – the main institution of memory politics combining research, educational and prosecutorial functions) have declared many times that cultivating the memory of 'cursed soldiers' is the institute's priority. The right wing incorporates popular culture by, for example, supporting nationalist rappers to popularise 'the cursed soldiers' (Majewski, 2021).

However, despite its central role in the symbolic politics of PiS, the commemoration of 'cursed soldiers' has not been subjected to a comprehensive analysis. In general, research to date on the growing popularity of nationalist and populist movements has paid relatively little attention to the use of historical memory to mobilise support, focusing instead on relative economic deprivation or responses to migration (Couperus et al., 2022). For example, the conventional wisdom is that the socially and economically excluded who were the 'losers' of the post-1989 economic transition voted for PiS (Jaskulowski & Kilias, 2016). It is hard to deny that the social agenda contributed to PiS's electoral victory and that it met the interests of economically disadvantaged groups. At the same time, the notion that this success can only be explained in terms of the support of 'losers' reflects the naïve liberal and leftist belief that nationalism is some aberration or epiphenomenon that will disappear as material conditions improve. However, nationalists mobilised the support of various social groups for whom issues of identity, a sense of 'being at home', and national pride were as important as economic motivations.

Research focused mainly on the history of the PPP itself and began back in the People's Republic of Poland (Polska Republika Ludowa, PRL), but it was subject to party censorship then (e.g. Blum, 1968; Góra & Halaba, 1967). It was not until the political transformation that the possibility of free research on the PPP opened up (Wnuk, 2000). After 1989, the partisans' own memoirs and various journalistic and popular science works also began to be published (e.g. Broński, 2015; Solak, 2015; Ślaski, 2012). Although censorship has been lifted, PPP historiography has been dominated by right-wing historians who adopt a nationalist paradigm of historical research. They focus on military history and political history, documenting the heroic achievements of male partisans and their persecution by the communists (e.g. Golik et al., 2017; Krajewski & Łobuszewski, 2017; Ostapiuk, 2019). Among the exceptions are works such as Mariusz Mazur's (2019) book, which analyses the everyday life of the partisans and their attitude towards national minorities.

Relatively little attention, however, has been paid to the analysis of the commemoration of the PPP. A book by Marta Kurkowska-Budzan (2009), which analysed the memories of veterans, should be mentioned here. The work is interesting in that it was written before the intensification of memory politics and the consolidation of the heroic image of the PPP. Anna Moroz analysed press and Internet discourses in the context of the Polish-Belarusian dispute over the memory of Rajmund Rajs 'Bury', who is responsible for ethnic cleansing (Moroz, 2016). A more comprehensive attempt to explain the origins of the memory politics of 'cursed soldiers' is the article by Kornelia Kończal (2020). Yet, the article overlooks the broader historical context of military communist nationalism and does not address the grassroots reception of memory politics. In this context, the article by Marije Hristova and Monika Żychlińska (2020), which goes beyond top-down discourse analysis by referring to participant observation, is interesting. The authors focus on volunteers participating in exhumation work at a military cemetery in Warsaw. There is no work analysing the memory politics of the 'cursed soldiers' in a comprehensive way that also takes into account the incorporation of popular culture and a broad bottom-up perspective. Our book therefore fills a gap in research on nationalist memory politics in Poland by providing a theoretically grounded systematic case study that takes into account the reception of this politics.

Methodology

The book relies on two types of data: existing data and data collected during the qualitative research. The former includes websites of various memory politics institutions, statements by politicians, newspaper articles, memoirs, films, murals, museum exhibitions, video clips, and blogs. We use existing data to reconstruct the top-down memorial discourse, but we also supplement it with data from participant observation and interviews. We understand discourse as a language-based way of constructing meaning in a signifying process. In line with the semiotic tradition, we define language broadly as a system of signs in the wide sense, not limited solely to its linguistic form. Discourse is a set of utterances providing language to talk about a given object or process at a particular historical moment (Hall, 2017). Discourse is inextricably linked to ideology, which means that the language construction is not so much a neutral description of a reality that exists 'out there', but a construct entangled in power relations.

The qualitative research consists of individual semi-structured interviews, group interviews, observation, and participatory observation. We rely on 160 interviews with different categories of interviewees who, to varying degrees, have participated in the production and realisation of memory politics, are involved in commemorating or contesting the commemoration of 'cursed soldiers', or are its recipients and consumers. The interviews included employees of memory politics institutions, politicians, local government officials, history teachers, social activists, informants belonging to national minorities, especially the Belarusian minority in Podlasie, and consumers of memory politics, e.g. those wearing so-called 'patriotic clothing', or passive recipients of the memory politics.

We used semi-structured interviews because this is a flexible technique combining open and closed questions. This technique allows a prepared list of specific questions to be asked, which makes it possible to collect comparable data. At the same time, interviewees have the opportunity to raise topics that are important to them (Brinkmann & Kvale, 2018). By qualitative research standards, our sample size is large, ensuring that we have achieved theoretical saturation. Our sample selection was also guided by the maximum diversity principle, so interviewees varied in terms of age, gender, occupation, place of residence, and education. Interviewees agreed to participate in the study and to use the interviews for research purposes on condition of confidentiality and anonymity. Maintaining confidentiality and anonymity is important since some interviewees, especially those who spoke critically about the PPP, feared that revealing their identity could harm them or their relatives. We also conducted seven group interviews with young interviewees, most of whom were not involved in the commemoration of the 'cursed soldiers', but constituted a potential audience. Each group interview involved between a few and a dozen interviewees. Group interviews provide insights into what people say in semi-public situations, reflecting the dynamics of real social situations (Stewart & Shamdasani, 2014).

The book also draws on data obtained during observation and participatory observation. We understand participant observation broadly as including informal interviews, both individual and group, which occur spontaneously during shared participation in various events. Between 2020 and 2023, we participated in numerous public and semi-public events such as festivals, conferences, ceremonies, sports competitions, lectures, historical re-enactments, music concerts, theatre performances, and demonstrations. We visited various museums, exhibitions, and memorials in different cities and towns. The research also included the production of photographic and audiovisual documentation (Blee, 2007; Jerolmack & Khan, 2017; Pilkington, 2016).

Structure and Line of Argumentation

Excluding the first introductory chapter, the book consists of five chapters. In the second chapter, we discuss our theoretical starting point. Referring to the constructivist paradigm, we present our understanding of nationalism and distinguish between different types. We argue that the ideology of PiS is an example of an exclusionary and authoritarian version of nationalism. We explain our understanding of collective memory, defining it in terms of a dynamic process of communication and reception entangled in power relations, taking place under conditions of hegemonic memory structures. We then present our understanding of hegemony, introducing the notion of a key memory symbol and a collective emotional field. We also refer to the modified model of decoding hegemonic content and discuss the emotional dimension of engagement in reception.

The third chapter deals with the origins of the memory politics of the 'cursed soldiers'. To provide historical context, we briefly discuss the history of the PPP itself. We briefly examine communist memory politics, challenging the conventional wisdom that in the PRL the PPP was portrayed unequivocally negatively and as doomed to oblivion. We then explain how and why the right wing transformed the PPP into a symbol of 'cursed soldiers'. In the fourth chapter, we study the process of the takeover of the symbol of 'cursed soldiers' by PiS. We demonstrate how the party elevated 'cursed soldiers' to the status of a key memorial symbol in its hegemonic project. We analyse how the party uses memory politics to construct symbolic national boundaries between us 'real' Poles and all the rest ('cursed soldiers' as the Polish nation). We also discuss the role of 'cursed soldiers' as an allegory of the fate of the Polish nation in the context of the discourse of two totalitarianisms, two Holocausts, and a competition for suffering.

The next (fifth) chapter centres on an examination of the reception of memory politics. Referring to a modified decoding/coding model, we focus on the meanings and emotions associated with the reception of the symbolism of 'cursed soldiers'. We unveil the main patterns of interpretations and types of experiencing in the context of hegemonic politics, presenting a kind of semiotic-emotional map of the grassroots reception of the symbolism of 'cursed soldiers' in Polish society. A relatively large amount of space is devoted to Belarusian interviewees whose historical experiences are in conflict with the hegemonic memory politics that venerates partisans carrying out ethnic cleansing in Podlasie.

The sixth and final chapter concludes our main findings in the context of our theoretical assumptions. We argue that the memory politics of the 'cursed soldiers' is embedded in the authoritarian nationalism of PiS. This politics constructs an exclusionary symbolic and emotional space in which there is no room for historical experience that does not fit into the hegemonic narrative. Hegemonic politics operates not only on the semiotic level but also on the emotional level by invoking exclusionary emotional criteria of national belonging. Yet, the hegemonic meaning of the symbolism of 'cursed soldiers' is susceptible to various interpretations and is also met with contestation. This creates the possibility of more agonistic memory politics, which, however, requires institutional support to increase the visibility and legitimacy of minority experiences in the public space.

References

Blee, K. M. (2007). Ethnographies of the far right. *Journal of Contemporary Ethnography*, *36*(2), 119–128.

Blum, I. (1968). *Z dziejów wojska polskiego 1944–1948 [From the history of the Polish army 1944–1948]*. Warsaw: MON.

Brinkmann, S., & Kvale, S. (2018). *Doing interviews*. London: Sage.

Broński "Uskok", Z. (2015). *Pamiętnik [Memoirs]*. Lublin and Warsaw: IPN.
Bull, A. C., & Hansen, H. L. (2016). On agonistic memory. *Memory Studies, 9*(4), 390–404.
Couperus, S., Tortola, P. D., & Rensmann, L. (2022). Memory politics of the far right in Europe. *European Politics and Society*. Advanced online publication. DOI: 10.1080/23745118.2022.2058757
Golik, D. et al. (2017). Żołnierze wyklęci [The cursed soldiers]. Warsaw: Volumen.
Góra, W., & Halaba, R. (Eds). (1967). *W walce o utrwalenie władzy ludowej w Polsce, 1944–1947 [The struggle for the consolidation of people's power in Poland, 1944–1947]*. Warsaw: Książka i Wiedza.
Hall, S. (2017). *The fateful triangle: Race, ethnicity, nation*. Cambridge, MA: Harvard University Press.
Hobsbawm, E., & Ranger, T. (Eds.). (1983). *The invention of tradition*. Cambridge: Cambridge University Press.
Hristova, M., & Żychlińska, M. (2020). Mass grave exhumations as patriotic retreat. *Human Remains and Violence, 6*(2), 42–60.
Jaskulowski, K., & Kilias, J. (2016). Polityka nacjonalistycznej rewolucji. *Studio Opinii*. Retrieved from http://studioopinii.pl/archiwa/164532
Jaskulowski, K., & Majewski, P. (2023). The memory politics of Cursed Soldiers, anti-semitism and racialisation. *Nations and Nationalism*. Advance online publication. DOI: 10.1111/nana.12937
Jaskulowski, K., Majewski, P., & Surmiak, A. (2022). *Teaching history, celebrating nationalism: School history education in Poland*. London and New York: Routledge.
Jerolmack, C., & Khan, S. (Eds.). (2017). *Approaches to ethnography*. Oxford: OUP.
Kończal, K. (2020). The invention of the 'Cursed Soldiers' and its opponents: Post-war partisan struggle in contemporary Poland. *East European Politics and Societies, 34*(1), 67–95.
Krajewski, K., & Łobuszewski, T. (Eds.). (2017). Żołnierze wyklęci 1944–1963. [The cursed soldiers 1944–1963]. Warsaw: IPN.
Kurkowska-Budzan, M. (2009). *Antykomunistyczne podziemie zbrojne na Białostocczyźnie [The anti-communist armed underground in the Białystok region]*. Cracow: Towarzystwo Wydawnicze "Historia Iagiellonica".
Majewski, P. (2021). *Rap w służbie narodu [Rap in the service of the nation]*. Warsaw: Scholar.
Mazur, M. (2019). *Antykomunistycznego Podziemia Portret Zbiorowy 1945–1956 [Anti-communist underground collective portrait 1945–1956]*. Warsaw: Bellona.
Moroz, A. (2016). *Między pamięcią a historią. Konflikt pamięci zbiorowych Polaków i Białorusinów na przykładzie postaci Rajmunda Rajsa "Burego" [Between memory and history: Conflict of collective memories of Poles and Belarusians on the example of Rajmund Rajs "Bury"]*. Warsaw: IPN.
Ostapiuk, M. (2019). *Komendant "Bury". Biografia kpt. Romualda Adama Rajsa "Burego" (1913–1949) [Commander "Bury": Biography of Capt. Romuald Adam Rajs "Bury" (1913–1949)]*. Białystok: IPN.
Pilkington, H. (2016). *Loud and proud: Passions and politics in the English Defence League*. Manchester: Manchester University Press.
Solak, A. (2015). *Krucjata wyklętych [The crusade of the cursed]*. Cracow: eSPe.
Stewart, D. W., & Shamdasani, P. N. (2014). *Focus groups: Theory and practice*. London: Sage.

Szacki, J. (1991). *Dylematy historiografii idei oraz inne studia i szkice [Dilemmas of the history of ideas and other studies and sketches]*. Warsaw: PWN.
Śląski, J. (2012). Żołnierze wyklęci [Cursed soldiers]. Warsaw: Rytm.
Wnuk, R. (2000). Stosunek polskiej historiografii po roku 1989 do antykomunistycznego podziemia i opozycji demokratycznej [The attitude of Polish historiography after 1989 to the anti-communist underground and the democratic opposition]. In P. Kosiewski, & G. Motyka (Eds.), *Historycy polscy i ukraińscy wobec problemów XX wieku [Polish and Ukranian historians and the problems of the 20th century]* (pp. 49–60). Cracow: Universitas.

2 Nationalism, Hegemony, and Memory Politics

Defining Nationalism

The study of nationalism has traditionally focused on the processes of nation-building (Jaskulowski, 2009; Özkirimli, 2010; Smith, 1998). Modernists have claimed that nations are a corollary of modernising processes such as democratisation or industrialisation (Gellner, 1983; Hobsbawm, 1990). Ethnosymbolists have argued that nations evolved gradually through a long process from premodern ethnic groups (Smith, 1986). Modernists and ethnosymbolists have disagreed on the origins and continuity of nations but have shared a similar perspective on nations and focused on macro-analyses of enduring and long historical processes (Billig, 1995; Edensor, 2002). It was constructivists who proposed going beyond historical discussions about the origins and beyond the attempt to find a universal causal theory explaining the origins of nation-states. Instead, they focused on the everyday production and reproduction of nations understood in dynamic and processual terms (Billig, 1995; Brubaker, 2004; Edensor, 2002). A constructivist approach to nationalism is our theoretical starting point (Jaskulowski, 2019). However, we do not refer to any specific theory of nationalism, but, drawing on authors such as Billig (1995), Brubaker (2004), and Hall (2017), we make some assumptions that we understand as sensitising concepts (Blumer, 1954).

We assume that a nation is not so much a coherent and enduring social group as a politically significant construct, a correlate of nationalism understood as a signifying practice entangled in power relations. Nations are not really existing and clearly bounded sociological entities, some kind of social Ding an sich, with permanent and stable identities, but are produced by nationalist cultural, discursive, and affective practices (Bonikowski, 2016). Nationalism constructs social reality as naturally divided into distinct nations that are regarded as the only legitimate source of political power. It interpellates individuals as homo nationalists, proclaiming that national affiliation is second nature for the individual (Balibar, 2002; Jaskulowski & Majewski, 2016, 2020). The category of nation refers to a dynamic process of assigning meanings to social reality, which is subject to constant contestation and negotiation in everyday life taking place under conditions of hegemonic structures (Hall, 2017).

Depending on how nationalisms define the nation, different types of this ideology can be distinguished. The classical Hans Kohn (1944) typology, reproduced to this day in many works, assumed that there are two basic types, namely civic nationalism (often identified with Western Europe) and ethnic nationalism (conventionally attributed to Eastern Europe) (Jaskulowski, 2010; Kohn, 1944). It is argued that civic nationalism defines the nation in purely political terms and is characterised by inclusiveness, democracy, and liberalism, while ethnic nationalism imagines the nation as a cultural or ethnic community (these two factors are often equated) that is exclusionary and authoritarian. This civic/ethnic dichotomy has repeatedly been criticised on a number of different grounds (Brubaker, 2004; Jaskulowski, 2010; Kuzio, 2002). For example, it has been argued that the dichotomy idealises Western Europe and negatively stereotypes Eastern Europe, that civic nationalism also has cultural components or that it has an irrational dimension (Jaskulowski, 2016). The popularity of this dichotomy likely stems in part from that it points to an important fact, namely that nationalisms differ significantly from each other and have different consequences for communities and individuals (e.g. some are supportive of stable democratic governments, others are the basis for dictatorships and ethnic cleansing).

Liah Greenfeld (1992) argues that the differences between nationalisms basically amount to two issues: the understanding of the nature of national sovereignty, which can be imagined in two ways either in individualistic or collective terms, and the definition of national membership, which can be seen as being dependent on, or independent of, the will of individuals. Greenfeld, like the classical approaches, assumed that if nationalism defines national belonging in cultural terms (as opposed to political conceptions of the nation), it has the potential to be exclusionary. However, all nationalism contains a cultural component, and the inclusiveness of nationalism does not depend on whether it defines national belonging in cultural terms, but on how it defines culture as a criterion for national belonging (Kymlicka, 2001). Nationalism may define cultural conditions of belonging in such a way that they are relatively easy to fulfil (e.g. a new language can be learned) or difficult or impossible (e.g. one must not only learn the language but speak without a foreign accent and change one's religion). Nationalisms can also refer to ethnic (birth) or physiological criteria conceiving national belonging as determined. To the aforementioned two criteria, one more must be added, i.e. how relations between nations are imagined. The image of these relations can stretch between two extreme poles: international relations can be seen as a Hobbesian state of nature, i.e. the war of all against all, or as a solidarity-based and peaceful international order. These criteria do not warrant a classification of nationalisms sensu stricto (i.e. they are not exhaustive). Nationalism seems too diverse a phenomenon to put into any rigid and schematic framework, but these criteria will help to structure the empirical material and characterise PiS's understanding of the nation.

Authoritarian Exclusionary Nationalism

The PiS ideology fits into the collectivist approach, since for the party sovereignty is an attribute of the Polish nation, imagined as an inherently organic entity, superior to the individual. Such an understanding of sovereignty gives rise to a tendency to restrict individual rights in the name of the good of the nation. Thus, the party's 2005 draft of a new constitution confined civic rights and freedoms and allowed for their suspension in favour of the vague category of the common good (Jaskulowski, 2012). The draft was never implemented because PiS never had a constitutional majority, but after forming the government in 2015, it adopted a number of measures to weaken the protection of civil rights. For example, it increased the police's powers of surveillance of citizens, limited freedom of assembly and freedom of speech, reduced the autonomy of the judiciary, and subordinated the Constitutional Tribunal to the party (Sadurski, 2019).

PiS assumes that the nation is a cohesive and organic community that has some kind of singular national will, which is not necessarily the sum of individual citizen preferences. Rather, certain groups, in particular, are positioned to express this will. Nationalist order understood in this way is a political system based on Schmitt's principle of national majority (Schmitt, 1985). Political subjectivity is granted only to the 'healthy' part of the nation, which exercises physical and moral tyranny over the rest of the nation. PiS does not govern on behalf of a numerical majority, but on behalf of real and common Poles. It governs in accordance with authentic traditions, which a large part of the nation does not understand because it has been manipulated by cosmopolitan liberal elites tainted by the 'treason gene'. 'Proper' national consciousness has yet to be instilled in Poles by a nationalist vanguard, a genuine national elite to replace the liberal 'liar-elites' (Bill, 2022). Poles need to be re-educated – the reform of school education, the educational activities of the IPN, and the memory politics of the 'cursed soldiers' serve this purpose. And 'half-Poles' need to be disciplined, e.g. sexual minority activists need to be harassed, women's reproductive rights confined, etc. (Gwiazda, 2021; Walicki, 2011).

The conviction that the nation is an inherently solidary and homogeneous group is accompanied by a tendency to treat conflict in terms of conspiracies organised by various internal and external enemies. PiS frames its critics not so much as equal political opponents but as national renegades, situating them outside the national community. It accuses them of treason and undermines their legitimacy to take part in public life. It continues the traditions of Polish integral nationalism of the National Democracy (Narodowa Demokracja) of the late 19th and early 20th centuries. While for the National Democracy it was the Jews who inspired action against Poland, PiS does not evoke a single fixed enemy. PiS does not refer to any coherent conspiracy theory using a more flexible rhetoric of suspicion, which allows it to react to changing circumstances. Depending on the situation, the enemy could be Germans, Russians, Brussels, the left, women, or LGBTQ. The allusive rhetoric of PiS has an often religious tone, suggesting that behind all conspiracies there is some transcendent force – a civilisation of death waging a metaphysical war against the civilisation of life, of which Catholic Poland is the embodiment.

PiS defines the uniqueness of the Polish nation in terms of its historical links with Catholicism. The origins of the melding of Polish nationalism with Catholicism must be sought in the 19th century and then the early 20th century when Polish integral nationalists recognised that Catholicism was the inherent basis of Polishness (Dmowski, 1927; Porter-Szűcs, 2017). As Geneviève Zubrzycki (2006) shows, the period of the PRL was also formative. A large part of Polish society did not treat the communist state as their own and did not recognise those in power as Poles. The communists strenuously emphasised the Polishness of the state by evoking, for example, the myth of a return to the 'natural' pre-Polish early medieval borders (Thum, 2011; Zaremba, 2006). However, under conditions of rivalry between the state and the Catholic Church, and dependence on the Soviet Union, this strategy enjoyed only partial success. In such a situation, Polishness began to be identified even more strongly with Catholicism. Not only did the Catholic Church present itself as the most important defender of 'real' Polishness, but it also adapted the romantic mythology that Poles were entrusted by providence with the mission to redeem the sins of the Western world.

As a result of the democratic transition, there was a change in the relationship between the nation, the state, and the Church, as the state was no longer seen as 'foreign', and the Church had lost its former status as a major independent institution. As a consequence, the link between Catholicism and national identity lost its self-evidence and became weakened, which the Church and the right wing began to frame in moralistic terms as a crisis of Polishness. PiS is therefore trying by giving new meaning to religious-national myths. And so it resuscitated the stereotype of the Pole-Catholic or the myth of Poland as the bulwark of Christianity. In the rhetoric of PiS, the line between what is national and what is religious is blurred, and the party attempts to subordinate law and public life to Catholic doctrine. A prominent example of the latter was the tightening of anti-abortion laws by the Constitutional Court, which triggered mass protests by women in Poland (Hall, 2019).

The nation in the nationalist construction of reality never exists in isolation but is always surrounded by other nations. An important element that differentiates nationalisms is therefore how they conceive of relations between nations. The nationalism of PiS fits into the National Democracy tradition of defining international relations as a sphere for the pursuit of egoistic interests by nation-states, in which inevitable conflict is inscribed. The party evokes a narcissistic image of Poland as a country that is the target of constant hostile conspiracies. In keeping with the National Democratic tradition enlivened by communist propaganda, the main antagonist is the German state, which has continuously pursued a Drang nach Osten politics. Germany allegedly conceived the project of European integration in order to subjugate Europe economically. Referring to the romantic and insurrectionist tradition, PiS also considers Russia to be a dangerous enemy. According to the party, Russia killed the Polish president in an assassination in Smoleńsk, and the invasion of Ukraine confirms that it is capable of such criminal actions. The cynical vision of international relations creates an atmosphere of danger, which is further fuelled by the Huntingtonian discourse of a clash of civilisations between Europe and the Islamic world. This discourse creates a sense of crisis and is intended to legitimise various emergency actions restricting civil rights, e.g. the introduction of a state of emergency in north-eastern Poland in response to irregular crossing of the Polish-Belarusian border by refugees (Klaus & Szulecka, 2022).

In defining national belonging PiS refers mainly to a specifically understood national culture, which it conceives of in a metaphorically speaking 'thick' way, as an essential and autonomous entity deeply rooted in history, homogeneous and inextricably linked to Catholicism. Defining Polishness in terms of 'thick' culture implies drawing rigid divisions into 'us' and 'them'. The other side of this image of a 'thick' homogeneous culture is the implied existence of an 'other' culture, which is often presented as a threat to 'our' identity. Representatives of this threatening culture become various 'others': foreigners, immigrants, refugees, etc. The essentialisation of national culture leads to the formation of impassable barriers between people and thus performs similar functions to the concept of race by taking the form of cultural racism. However, this cultural racism is characterised by a tendency to transform into biological racism, which was particularly evident in the rhetoric of moral panic against refugees from the Middle East and North Africa during the refugee rights crisis of 2015–2016. In the discourse of PiS, the visible signifier of the cultural otherness of refugees became their dark skin colour (Jaskulowski, 2019).

However, Polish right-wing nationalism is not an example of a pure ethnic ideology. Rather, we are dealing here with a combination of two principles for determining national belonging: the aforementioned deterministic and voluntaristic. For the right wing, the sole 'proper' ethnicity or skin colour is not a sufficient condition to be considered a 'real' Pole – one still has to identify with the right-wing version of Polishness and the right-wing political project. The proper ethnic origin is also not always a necessary condition. Sometimes foreign origin or skin colour can be 'forgiven' through a neophyte commitment to a right-wing project. However, at any time nationalists can remind new members of the nation of their foreign origins and exclude them from the nation if the neophytes are not sufficiently zealous.

Nationalism and Collective Memory

Nationalist theorists unanimously stress that the construction of a shared collective memory serves as an important instrument of nation-building (Gellner, 1983; Hobsbawm, 1990; Smith, 1999). In the case of Polish nationalism, references to the past have always been of great importance, which can also be seen in the case of PiS nationalism, which emphasises the historical distinctiveness of the Polish nation. Scholars writing about the significance of the past have used a variety of terms ('memories', 'myths', 'invented traditions', 'traditions', 'collective memory', etc.). This terminological diversity adds to the difficulty of defining the concept of collective memory, with challenges such as clarifying the connection linking collective and individual aspects, alongside differentiating history from memory. Thus, although the literature on 'collective memory' is growing, there is still no agreed definition of the term (Jaskulowski & Majewski, 2020; Kansteiner, 2002; Szacki, 2011; Wertsch & Roediger, 2008).

As Kansteiner (2002) noted, there are two strands in defining the concept of collective memory. First, the concept can refer to socially shared representations of the past, which are often objectified in the form of various artefacts relating to the past. The second approach focuses on the different practices of memory production and reception. Referring to critical media theory, as with our approach to nationalism, we combine these two perspectives. We understand collective memory, on the one hand, as an objectified representation of the past, and on the other hand as a complex and dynamic process of the production and reception of these objectified representations. We look at collective memory as a dynamic process of communication that takes place under conditions of dominant memory structures that simultaneously shape and are shaped by everyday mnemonic practices (Jaskulowski & Majewski, 2020). Paraphrasing Marx, it can be said that people make their own collective memory, but they do not do so as they please; they do so not under self-chosen circumstances but within pre-existing memory structures that are stabilised by hegemonic collective memory projects. This processual approach allows us to see that individuals and various mnemonic agents can modify or contest hegemonic conceptions of collective memory according to their own interests, identities, or experiences (Hall, 1980; Ryan, 2011).

Hegemony and Emotions

We assume that certain social actors have a greater ability to impose their construction of social reality, including their conception of the nation. We define the concept of hegemony in a non-essentialist and non-reductionist way, without assuming a priori that certain factors are decisive (Hall, 2017). In the context of memory politics, the control of state power is of great importance. By controlling public education, the calendar of official

Nationalism, Hegemony, and Memory Politics 15

ceremonies and museums, the rulers have the tools to enforce and reinforce the hegemonic version of collective memory and to marginalise other memories. Hegemonic memory projects take the form of complex narratives that redefine the national past: highlighting new turning points, a new chronology, a new set of national heroes, etc. At the same time, the hegemonic memory politics constructs a new set of symbols to represent these complex narratives. In this context, particularly important are the key memory symbols that structure, organise, and condense the entire complex of project-specific meanings (Ortner, 1973).

Key memory symbols perform cognitive, emotional, and behavioural functions in hegemonic projects. Cognitively, they represent complex narratives and abstract concepts in simple, concrete, and easy-to-understand ways, referring to familiar and everyday experiences. Such simple and tangible symbols provide mental access to more complex conceptual constructs, such as the notion of the nation (Anderson, 1991) or the concept of national history (Jaskulowski, 2016). For example, the idea of sacrifice in the name of an abstract nation is often illustrated with the figure of a soldier dying in defence of the motherland, depicted as a crying mother. Because of their emotional resonance (the nation as a crying mother), such symbols motivate people to take action, such as voting for a political party that promises to defend the nation. Key memory symbols condense a whole range of different meanings providing an abbreviated, concrete, and emotional way of evoking more complex narratives easily understood by the recipients.

Symbolic anthropology assumes that certain symbols are central to given communities and organise the whole cultural system (Ortner, 1973). Such an account, however, is too static and totalising, as it takes too little account of the dynamism and entanglement in the power relations of collective memory. Therefore, we understand the key symbol of collective memory more dynamically and processually as a tool and effect of hegemonic struggle. Its meaning is stabilised by the dominant ideology but is always open to contestation. We define the key symbol of memory as being central to a particular ideology rather than to the cultural system as a whole. From this perspective, we look at the 'cursed soldiers', who, we argue, have been elevated to the status of a key symbol of collective memory in the right-wing project. However, as we will show later in the book, the acceptance of 'cursed soldiers' as a key symbol of memory cannot be taken for granted.

We understand hegemony more broadly than in the classic Gramscian approach as encompassing not only the production of dominant cultural meanings that become institutionalised and objectified in various cultural practices and artefacts but also as the generation of affects and, above all, dominant collective emotions. By affects we mean basic feelings, the feeling that one is feeling, bodily sensations that vary in the degree to which they are perceived as pleasurable and the degree of arousal (Ahmed, 2004; Barrett & Russell, 2015; Massumi, 1995). Traditionally, it was assumed that affects are the basis of emotions, which have a universal biological foundation and are accompanied by universal physiological distinctive signs (e.g. the emotion of sadness is accompanied by a characteristic facial expression). However, the constructivist approach demonstrates that emotions are more complex and cannot be easily reduced to universal patterns that have biological underpinnings. As we assume following constructivist theories, emotions have a socially and culturally conditioned character, i.e. they acquire meaning only in social situations, they exist only between people, and the ways of experiencing and expressing them are socially and culturally conditioned. People can express and interpret bodily experiences of pleasure or unpleasure very differently depending on the cultural context or their pool of concepts distinguishing different types of emotions. People make sense of their embodied experiences and expressions in the course of social interaction in the context of social recognition of emotions by others. Emotions are therefore social in nature; they are not only conditioned by society but also manifest in the interactions among people (Ahmed, 2004).

In the context of collective emotions, we refer to social psychology literature, which talks about the 'collective emotional field', i.e. collective emotions experienced as objectively existing 'out there' at the level of the social system (De Rivera et al., 2007; Solak et al., 2012). For example, late-capitalist societies are dominated by an economic discourse based on a neoliberal understanding of society. This discourse, institutionalised in the counselling and coaching industry, constructs individuals as economic agents who are self-responsible and self-entrepreneurial. It frames the lives of individuals as a succession of individual achievements dependent solely on their own efforts, which must be constantly made in order to achieve more success. It simultaneously generates conditions for certain affective and emotional reactions. It creates, for example, the conditions for feeling pleasure and arousal accompanying professional success, which translates into more complex emotions, which are given meaning by the neoliberal discourse. And so it prompts individuals to feel pride in these supposedly self-made achievements and reluctance or even contempt for those individuals who fail in the free market (Jaskulowski & Pawlak, 2022). In a word, as social psychologists argue, societies tend to create an emotional field that is objectified in various cultural artefacts and social institutions that encourage audiences to experience and express certain emotions. If this field is permanent, i.e. if the conditions generating the emotions in question last over time, then people acquire a relatively permanent predisposition to express certain emotions more often than others, and so, one can say, a certain emotional habitus develops, which becomes, metaphorically speaking, a bridge between the macro-level constituted by the hegemonic emotional field and the micro level, i.e. the emotional responses of the individual.

However, the concept of the collective emotional field needs some refinement in line with our more processual approach. Thus, we define the collective emotional field not so much as a product of society as such, but as an effect of various ideologies competing for hegemony. As we wrote during the 2015–2016 refugee rights crisis, PiS framed Muslim refugees as spreaders of dangerous contagious diseases and terrorists whose goal is to Islamise Poland. It evoked a sense of danger and fear, which it used as a tool of social control and political mobilisation. This emotional message had specific cognitive functions, reinforcing the party's ideological message, as it motivated people to perceive reality according to anti-Muslim perceptions, e.g. to select information in such a way that it confirms the dominant image of the Muslim terrorist. Thus, emotions not only push people to act but also perform cognitive functions, influencing, for example, the choice of preferred media. Unlike social psychologists, we assumed that the emotional field is rarely completely stable, uniform, and subordinated to a single ideology. The collective emotional field is always susceptible to negotiation and contestation, as shown, for example, by the aforementioned refugee rights protection crisis. Although a sense of danger and fear dominated, other emotions were also evident in the public space. For example, a few left-wing politicians appealed for empathy for refugees and expressed anger at racist anti-Muslim propaganda (Jaskulowski, 2019).

References

Ahmed, S. (2004). *The politics of emotions*. Edinburgh: Edinburgh University Press.
Anderson, B. (1991). *Imagined communities: Reflections on the origin and spread of nationalism*. London: Verso.
Balibar, É. (2002). *Politics and the other scene*. London: Verso.
Barrett, L. F., & Russell, J. A. (Eds.). (2015). *The psychological construction of emotion*. New York: Guilford.
Bill, S. (2022). Counter-elite populism and civil society in Poland: PiS's strategies of elite replacement. *East European Politics and Societies: And Cultures, 36*(1), 118–140.
Billig, M. (1995). *Banal nationalism*. London: Sage.
Blumer, H. (1954). What is wrong with social theory? *American Sociological Review, 19*(1), 3–10.
Bonikowski, B. (2016). Nationalism in settled times. *Annual Review of Sociology, 42*(1), 427–449.
Brubaker, R. (2004). *Ethnicity without groups*. Cambridge, MA: Harvard University Press.
De Rivera, J., Kurrien, R., & Olsen, N. (2007). The emotional climate of nations and their culture of peace. *Journal of Social Issues, 63*, 255–271.
Dmowski, R. (1927). *Naród, państwo, Kościół [Nation, state, the Church]*. Warsaw: Obóz Wielkiej Polski.
Edensor, T. (2002). *National identity, popular culture and everyday life*. Oxford: Berg
Gellner, E. (1983). *Nations and nationalism*. Oxford: Blackwell.
Greenfeld, L. (1992). *Nationalism: Five roads to modernity*. Cambridge, MA: Harvard University Press.

Gwiazda, A. (2021). Right-wing populism and feminist politics: The case of Law and Justice in Poland. *International Political Science Review*, *42*(5), 580–595.
Hall, B. (2019). Gendering resistance to right-wing populism: Black Protest and a new wave of feminist activism in Poland? *American Behavioral Scientist*, *63*(10), 1497–1515.
Hall, S. (1980). Encoding/decoding. In S. Hall, D. Hobson, A. Lowe, & P. Willis (Eds.), *Culture, media, language* (pp. 128–138). London: Hutchinson.
Hall, S. (2017). *The fateful triangle: Race, ethnicity, nation*. Cambridge, MA: Harvard University Press.
Hobsbawm, E. J. (1990). *Nations and nationalism since 1780: Programme, myth, reality*. Cambridge, MA: Cambridge University Press.
Jaskulowski, K. (2009). *Nacjonalizm bez narodów [Nationalism without nations]*. Wrocław: Monografie FNP.
Jaskulowski, K. (2010). Western (civic) versus Eastern (ethnic) nationalism: The origins and critique of the dichotomy. *Polish Sociological Review*, *171*, 289–303.
Jaskulowski, K. (2012). *Wspólnota symboliczna [Symbolic community]*. Gdańsk: WN Katedra.
Jaskulowski, K. (2016). The magic of the national flag. *Ethnic and Racial Studies*, *39*, 557–573.
Jaskulowski, K. (2019). *The everyday of politic of the migration crisis in Poland*. Cham: Palgrave.
Jaskulowski, K., & Majewski, P. (2016). The UEFA European football championship 2012 and pop nationalism in Poland. *Identities*, *23*, 555–571.
Jaskulowski, K., & Majewski, P. (2020). Politics of memory in Upper Silesian schools: Between Polish homogeneous nationalism and its Silesian discontents. *Memory Studies*, *13*(1), 60–73.
Jaskulowski, K., & Pawlak, M. (2022). Middling migrants, neoliberalism and racism. *Journal of Ethnic and Migration Studies*, *48*(9), 2056–2072.
Kansteiner, W. (2002). Finding meaning in memory: A methodological critique of collective memory studies. *History and Theory*, *41*(2), 179–197.
Klaus, W., & Szulecka, M. (2022). Departing or being deported? Poland's approach towards humanitarian migrants. *Journal of Refugee Studies*. Advanced online publication. DOI: 10.1093/jrs/feac063
Kohn, H. (1944). *The idea of nationalism. A study in its origins and background*. New York: The Macmillan Company.
Kuzio, T. (2002). The myth of the civic state: A critical survey of Hans Kohn's framework for understanding nationalism. *Ethnic and Racial Studies*, *1*, 20–39.
Kymlicka, W. (2001). *Politics in the vernacular: Nationalism, multiculturalism, and citizenship*. Oxford: Oxford University Press.
Massumi, B. (1995). The autonomy of affect. *Cultural Critique*, *31*, 83–103.
Ortner, S. B. (1973). On key symbols. *American Anthropologists*, *75*(5), 1338–1346.
Özkirimli, U. (2010). *Theories of nationalism: A critical introduction*. New York: Palgrave.
Porter-Szűcs, B. (2017). The birth of the Polak-katolik. *Sprawy Narodowościowe*, *49*, 1–12.
Ryan, L. (2011). Memory, power and resistance: The anatomy of a tripartite relationship. *Memory Studies*, *4*(2), 154–169.
Sadurski, W. (2019). *Poland's constitutional*. Oxford: Oxford University Press.

Schmitt, C. (1985). *The crisis of parliamentary*. Cambridge, MA: MIT Press.
Smith, A. D. (1986). *The ethnic origins of nations*. Oxford: Blackwell.
Smith, A. D. (1998). *Nationalism and modernism: A critical survey of recent theories of nations and nationalism*. London and New York: Routledge.
Smith, A. D. (1999). *Myths and memories of the nation*. Oxford: Oxford University Press.
Solak, N., Jost, J. T., Sümer, N., & Clore, G. L. (2012). Rage against the machine: The case for system-level emotions. *Social and Personality Psychology Compass, 6*, 674–690.
Szacki, J. (2011). *Tradycja [Tradition]*. Warsaw: WUW.
Thum, G. (2011). *Uprooted: How Breslau became Wrocław during the century of expulsions*. Princeton, NJ: Princeton University Press.
Walicki, A. (2011). The troubling legacy of Roman Dmowski. *Dialogue and Universalism, 21*(4), 91–119.
Wertsch, J. V., & Roediger, H. L., III. (2008). Collective memory: Conceptual foundations and theoretical approaches. *Memory, 16*(3), 318–326.
Zaremba, M. (2006). *Communism – Legitimacy – Nationalism*. Frankfurt am Main: Peter Lang.
Zubrzycki, G. (2006). *The crosses of Auschwitz: Nationalism and religion in postcommunist Poland*. Chicago, IL: Chicago University Press.

3 From Bandits to 'Cursed Soldiers'

Polish Post-war Underground

The PPP was not a Polish peculiarity but part of a wider phenomenon. After the defeat of the German army by the Soviets, resistance against the communists emerged in many countries of Central, Eastern, and Southern Europe (Gehler & Schriffl, 2020). There were also structurally similar guerrilla movements but directed against the fascist dictatorship, such as the Spanish Maquis who after Franco's victory in the civil war fled to France, where some joined the anti-Hitler resistance. After 1944 when the Germans began to withdraw from France, the Spanish partisans attempted to retake Spain but suffered defeat in the Val d'Arán in October 1944. The Maquis continued their guerrilla struggle by carrying out sabotages and attacks on military officers and politicians, but as a result of brutal repression the partisans were crushed; some were murdered or arrested, and others fled to France or Morocco. Their peak of activity was between 1945 and 1947, but some remained active until the 1960s (Marco, 2016).

The PPP mainly derived from the Polish Underground State fighting against the Nazi occupation. Politically, the Polish Underground State was a coalition and covered almost the entire political spectrum from left to right. Beyond its structures remained the communists and the fascist nationalists, who formed the National Armed Forces (Narodowe Siły Zbrojne, NSZ). The Polish Underground State was subordinate to the Polish government in exile in London, which was recognised by its Western allies as the legitimate Polish government. At its peak, it had nearly half a million men, and in its armed forces the Home Army (Armia Krajowa, AK) served about 340,000–360,000, of which about 60,000 men belonged to partisan units (Kochanski, 2012).

The Polish government in exile hoped for the liberation of Poland by the Western Allies. However, when it became clear that the Soviet Union would be the main military force in the pre-war Polish territories, it was decided that the AK would take up arms against the retreating German troops. This Operation Tempest culminated in the Warsaw Uprising, which was quashed by the

DOI: 10.4324/9781003368847-3
This chapter has been made available under a CC-BY-NC-ND 4.0 license.

Germans after two months of fighting (Borodziej, 2006). In some areas, the AK succeeded in driving the Germans out, sometimes in cooperation with the Red Army. However, the Soviets supported the Polish communists, who began to establish their own administration. After the fighting had ended, therefore, AK partisans were disarmed by the Red Army and conscripted into the communist-controlled Polish army or subjected to various repressions. Some AK partisans therefore did not lay down their arms and awaited further events. Repression also extended to the leaders of the Polish Underground State, who were invited to negotiations in March 1945, were kidnapped, and transported to the Soviet Union, where they were subjected to a show trial (Chmielarz et al., 2000).

Earlier in January 1945, the Commander-in-Chief, faced with the new geopolitical situation, had disbanded the AK. In May 1945, the Underground Parliament also called for the abandonment of the armed struggle against the communists and joining in the rebuilding of the country (Bojko, 2020). The Polish Underground State leadership decided to support Stanisław Mikołajczyk, former Prime Minister of the Polish government in exile and leader of the Polish People's Party (Polskie Stronnictwo Ludowe, PSL), who had returned to Poland. Mikołajczyk, with the support of the Western Allies, undertook negotiations with the communists that resulted in the formation of a coalition government. Mikołajczyk hoped that as a result of parliamentary elections, it would be possible to peacefully remove the communists from power, something that the majority of Polish society also hoped for (Paczkowski, 1994).

Faced with the new political situation, the leaders dissolved the PPP structures in July 1945. In their place, they established the underground Resistance Movement without War and Diversion 'Freedom and Independence' (Ruch Oporu bez Wojny i Dywersji 'Wolność i Niezawisłość', WiN; hegemonic memory politics rarely mentions its full name, leaving out the words 'without war and diversion'), which was to focus on propaganda and intelligence activities. WiN hoped that Poland's future would be decided by free elections and a peaceful agreement between the Western Allies and the Soviet Union (Wnuk, 2020). It advocated a democratic system but at the same time emphasised simultaneously emphasized the connection of Polishness with Catholicism, wanted to restore the pre-war eastern border, and appealed to anti-Semitism. It evoked the stereotype of Judeo-Communism, accusing Jews of seizing power and introducing communism in Poland (Leszczyński, 2019, p. 43; Tokarska-Bakir, 2017). WiN aimed to disband partisan units and stop the armed struggle, which only succeeded in parts of the country. Many partisans disobeyed orders, some felt it was necessary to continue fighting, others feared repression, and others were unable to adjust to civilian life (Mazur, 2019).

Beyond WiN, there were authoritarian nationalists who, after the defeat of the Warsaw Uprising, withdrew from the AK and founded their own organisation, the National Military Union (Narodowe Zjednoczenie Wojskowe, NZW). They wanted to build ethnically homogeneous state with a strong executive. The state was to assimilate the Slav minorities, to marginalise the Jews as radically other, and to encourage their emigration. There were also fascist nationalists who had their own organisation, the National Armed Forces – Polish Organisation (Narodowa Siły Zbrojne – Organizacja Polska, NSZ – OP) and strived to carry out a national revolution and establish a fascist dictatorship. Their largest grouping, the Swietokrzyska Brigade, made an agreement with the Germans and, under their protection, withdrew to Czechoslovakia and eventually entered the American occupation zone in Germany. The leaders decided that the outbreak of a world conflict was unlikely and disbanded the partisan units. However, many partisans joined the NZW. There were also a number of different autonomous organisations. According to various estimates, between 120,000 and 180,000 people were active in the PPP. About half of them originated from the AK and were active within WiN, while about 30,000–40,000 belonged to the authoritarian and fascist nationalist underground. Only a minority of underground members belonged to armed partisan units. At the peak of PA activity in 1945, there were around 300 different units, with the total number of partisans ranging from 13,000 to 17,000 (Wnuk, 2020).

The military activities of the underground were limited, with the partisans attacking prisons and militia stations to free arrested partisans, repressing communist activists. As we have written, the largest underground WiN organisation sought to disband the guerrilla units, yet it had limited control over local partisan units. There were conflicts between the various units on political grounds and competition for limited resources in the local areas. Partisans also exploited the local population, looting food and clothing, and killing people they suspected of collaborating with the communists. The partisans often held prejudices against national minorities, whom they accused of having pro-communist sympathies, leading them to raid Belarusian, Lithuanian, Slovakian, and Ukrainian villages and kill Jews (Mazur, 2019; Panz, 2015; Tokarska-Bakir, 2017). Some units operating in mixed-nationality areas carried out ethnic cleansing. For example, the unit of Romuald Rajs 'Bury', belonging to the NZW, burned six villages in Podlasie (north-eastern part of Poland) at the beginning of 1946, killing 49 people of Belarusian nationality, including women and children, and shot 30 Belarusian carters. Bury's actions fitted in with the authoritarian nationalists' programme of building an ethnically homogeneous state. In 2005, before PiS won the elections, the IPN (2005) concluded, as a result of an investigation, that these actions of 'Bury' were a crime bearing the mark of genocide.

After 1945, the ranks of the PPP began to shrink rapidly as a result of the formation of the provisional government in June of that year and the announcement of general elections, which gave hope for a peaceful removal of the communists from power. The consolidation of power by the communists after the fraudulent elections in 1947, the lack of prospects for international conflict and the subsequent amnesty led basically to the complete disintegration of the underground. In 1947, partisan units numbered only, it is estimated, about 1,000 partisans, and three years later there were 250–400 partisans hiding in the forests, forming groups of two or three, who were systematically arrested or killed by the communist security forces. After 1956, only six partisans were still hiding, the last of whom was killed by the militia in 1963 (Wnuk, 2020). In 1950, the Church also openly dissociated itself from the PPP, signing an agreement with the communist authorities that condemned 'criminal underground bands' (Raina, 1994, pp. 232–235).

In total, about 8,600 partisans were killed, and about 79,000 underground members were arrested (of whom about 24,000 were murdered or sentenced to death). About 12,000 soldiers of the Polish army, militia, and security forces were killed in the fighting, as well as about 1,000 Soviet soldiers. Approximately 10,000 civilians were killed during the fighting. The latter category was quite diverse and included party activists, Polish and national minorities, and people whom the partisans suspected of collaboration with the communists (Mazur, 2019; Wnuk, 2020). However, the casualty figures must be seen as preliminary, as research is still underway. Civilian casualty figures, in particular, are not very precise, as research on the PPP has been dominated by nationalist historians who focus on the military struggle of the partisans and their persecution by the communists, overlooking civilian victims of partisans.

Erased from Memory? Communist Memory Politics

The conventional wisdom says that the communists not only repressed the 'cursed soldiers' but sought to erase them from collective memory. The hegemonic discourse emphasises that the communists pursued a politics that, following Connerton (2008), can be described as the 'repressive erasure' characteristic of totalitarian regimes. However, the PRL period was not uniform. The memory erasure politics fit in with the communists' practice of burying partisans killed in battle or murdered in prison in secret places. Information about where the bodies were buried was not disclosed even to the closest family. It was not until the political transformation that it became possible to exhume and identify the bodies, which became one of the tasks of the IPN (Hristova & Żychlińska, 2020). However, it should be noted – which hegemonic discourse overlooks – that the communists used similar practices for civilian victims of partisans and for Jewish victims of the third phase of the Holocaust. One of the more telling cases is the concealment of the burial place of the victims of 'Bury'. Throughout the PRL, the authorities did not disclose where the 30 carters bodies were buried. The families did not discover the graves until 1994, and it was not until three years later that the authorities of democratic Poland agreed to exhume them and move them to a cemetery, while another two years passed while they waited for permission to erect a monument to them (Czykwin, 2011).

While fighting the underground, the communists simultaneously conducted a propaganda campaign and framed the PPP as a fascist movement at the service of imperialist powers. The underground was represented as a class enemy recruited from the privileged classes that fought against socialist reforms. Propaganda resorted to dehumanising rhetoric that legitimised brutal repression. Referring to our theoretical categories, we can say that the propaganda produced a collective emotional field of fear and threat from the capitalist West (Machejek, 1955/1965; Tomasik, 1994).

In 1956, in a wave of thaw, an amnesty was announced, as a result of which several thousand former partisans were released from prison. The party liberalised its approach to cultural policy, allowing artists greater freedom, but censorship was maintained. However, works started to be produced that departed from socialist-realist patterns, in which the subject of the post-war underground also featured, although it was not a significant theme. One should mention here the main film of the Polish film school, Andrzej Wajda's *Ashes and Diamonds*, which shows the story of a post-war AK partisan. The partisan was portrayed as a tragic figure that could arouse the audience's sympathy. Major changes took place in the 1960s, which was connected with the formation within the party of a faction of so-called 'partisans' centred around the then Minister of the Interior Mieczysław Moczar. Moczar gathered communists who had been in the communist partisans during the war. The Moczarists emphasised their military past, which would legitimise their claim to greater power in the party (Lesiakowski, 1998). They also stressed their contribution to the struggle against the PPP. At the same time, however, Moczar sought support among former AK partisans and even the NSZ. The Moczarists were influential in the formation of a militaristic patriarchal communist nationalism in the 1960s and 1970s (Polniak, 2011). This militaristic nationalism manifested itself in the cult of the army and partisans, and emphasis on the threat from West Germany. It made extensive use of mass culture: novels, memoirs, historical reports, the popular press, and film (Polniak, 2016, p. 54).

In the context of communist military nationalism, the practice of commemorating militiamen, soldiers, and security officers who had been killed during fights after the Second World War developed intensively. Commemorations emphasised the connection of the killed with the Polish nation and the continuity of the Polish state dating back to the early Middle Ages. In militaristic mass culture, the fight against the underground began to be framed as a tragic civil war, often describing it with the nationalist patriarchal kinship metaphor as a 'fratricidal struggle' (women were mainly depicted in supporting roles as secretaries or nurses). According to the nationalist logic, the tragedy of the fighting was that 'a Pole was shooting a Pole', which played down the involvement of the Soviet forces (Babczenko & Bolduan, 1969). The propaganda mainly presented the process of growing distrust between the communists and the AK, framing this as a lost opportunity for national unity. This fitted in with Moczar's attempts to win over former AK members. For example, the film *Colours of battle* (made in 1964, based on Moczar's novel) shows the AL and AK fighting together against the Germans. After the battle the AK unit leaves and one of the AL partisans says: 'Nice guys, it's a pity they're not coming with us' (Polniak, 2016).

The communists framed the fight against the PPP as a fratricidal civil war, which was also a way of emphasising their Polishness. The communists realised that a large part of the population perceived them as being dependent on the Soviet Union or even ethnically other and, as we have written, emphasised that they were Polish (Zaremba, 2006). Moczarists inscribed this nationalist politics with anti-Semitism, blaming the responsibility for Stalinist terror on the Jewish leadership of the UB. When striving for power in the party, they used anti-Semitic rhetoric by portraying themselves as 'real' Poles who were trying to limit Jewish influence in the party (Osęka, 2008). This pattern can also be seen in propaganda pieces dedicated to the fight against the PPP, which contrasted ordinary patriotic security offices with uprooted Jewish leadership (Wałach, 1971, pp. 8, 174). From the partisans' perspective, anti-Semitism may also have been the basis of attempts to win over former AK members and members of the nationalist-authoritarian underground.

In some propaganda pieces, one can even detect a certain admiration for the PPP. The authors obviously declared that the PPP was the enemy, but at the same time they described the fights with the underground in the convention of a masculine adventure expressing a kind of respect for the enemy: 'Our opponents were undoubtedly tough people, hardened in fighting and struggling against adversity, mentally resistant and dangerous, cunning' (Wałach, 1971, p. 220). In general, however, the propaganda portrayed the leaders of the underground in a negative way as being responsible for the outbreak of a fratricidal civil war destroying national unity, which the communists presented in terms of the highest value. Stalinist schemes were invoked here, depicting the leaders not only as a class enemy but also as driven by low motives and morally degenerate. However, this was not always the norm: the novel *The Peers*, for example, depicts a fictional cruel commander of a post-war 'band' who gets a second chance after being released from prison. He graduates in engineering and becomes a manager in a factory, turning into an exemplary worker who receives state honours. The book describes the moral dilemma of factory workers who have to decide whether a former 'bandit' can be accepted into the communist party (Grzymkowski, 1976).

Rank-and-file partisans were portrayed in a more mixed way. On the one hand, like the leaders, they were described as degenerates. For example, a propaganda novel depicts 'Inka' Danuta Siedzikówna (in contemporary right-wing memory politics, 'Inka' has become important icon of the PPP and she is portrayed in the convention of a secular saint) as a sadistic nurse killing wounded security service officers (Babczenko & Bolduan, 1969, p. 189).

The cruelty of the partisans was highlighted by the published photos of the bodies of killed militiamen and UB officers – a practice adopted after 1989 by right-wing publishers, who, in turn, revel in the bodies of the partisans. On the other hand, rank-and-file partisans were more often described in a more neutral light as working-class people 'who would like to break with the past, get honestly to work and study' (Babczenko & Bolduan, 1969, p. 223). It was emphasised that rank-and-file partisans often found themselves in 'bands' because they were intimidated and should be given a second chance. There was also a clear contrast between the post-AK underground and the NSZ, which were presented in unambiguously negative terms as Nazis.

However, this image of the PPP began to change in the early 1970s, which can be linked to the waning influence of the Moczarists in the party. A technocratic fraction oriented towards economic modernisation took power in the party. Propaganda began to be dominated by the rhetoric of economic success, but when it came to attitudes towards the PPP, there was a return to Stalinist patterns. The underground was more often portrayed in an unambiguously negative way by resorting to dehumanising rhetoric. In films, for example, anti-communist partisans appeared only as anonymous figures visible from afar who murder, rape, and rob (Polniak, 2016).

Even during the PRL period, there were voices in the party forum demanding a shift in attitude towards the underground. The aforementioned Moczar, at the 7th Plenum of the Central Committee of the Communist Party on 3 December 1980, emphasised the common ethnicity of both sides in the post-war conflict: 'Thousands of our opponents also died in this civil war. Let us remember – they were Poles too (…) Often, it was simply the logic of the struggle or even an accident that brought them to the other side' (Ślaski, 1981, p. 4). Jerzy Ślaski, who himself belonged to the post-war unit and served time in prison, spoke in a similar vein. After his release from prison, Ślaski worked as a journalist and editor and was also a member of the 'Pax' Association – an organisation founded by Bolesław Piasecki, leader of the pre-war fascist National Radical Camp (Jaskulowski & Majewski, 2022). After the Second World War, Piasecki joined up with the communists and founded 'Pax', which was to bring together Catholics who supported the communist government. Many former anti-communist partisans, including those belonging to the NSZ, found refuge in Pax (Kunicki, 2012; Przetakiewicz, 1994). As a former PAX member Pax member put it, the organisation became a 'Noah's Ark' for former underground members, including radical nationalists (Przetakiewicz et al., 2022). Paradoxically, although communist propaganda deprecated the National Radical Camp or the NSZ as Nazi, communists cooperated with former members of these organisations if they found them useful. Nationalists, meanwhile, saw in the PRL the realisation of the programme of a homogeneous ethnic state, and in the Soviet Union the guarantee of Poland's western borders. In 1981, Ślaski (1981) published an article entitled 'Cursed and Crossed Out. They, too, were Poles', in which

From Bandits to 'Cursed Soldiers' 27

he recalled partisans 'whose names and nicknames were cursed'. Śląski admonished the remembrance of post-war partisans and called for their fair assessment. The article was in tune with the nationalism of the Moczarists by emphasising that the partisans were Poles, unlike, as the article suggested, some of the Stalinist-era security officers. Śląski (1996) published a book after the political transformation entitled *Cursed Soldiers*, which popularised the term (Jaskulowski & Majewski, 2022).

Turning 'Bandits' into 'Cursed Soldiers'

It was not until the collapse of communism that open discussion, free research and commemoration of the PPP became possible (Kończal, 2020; Kurkowska-Budzan, 2009). In the early 1990s, the conservative Republican League (LR) also took an interest in commemorating the PPA. The LR organised an exhibition in the autumn of 1993 at the University of Warsaw dedicated to the anti-communist underground, and a few years later, with the support of the liberal-conservative government, the LR published a book – an album entitled *Cursed Soldiers* (Wąsowski & Żebrowski, 1999). In 2003, the most active members of the LR founded the We Remember Foundation, which set itself the goal of commemorating the PPP, working closely with the IPN. Members of the League were credited with inventing the term 'cursed soldiers', but as we have seen, a similar term was used back in the 1980s by Śląski (Jaskulowski & Majewski, 2022). More importantly, however, the LR gave the term 'cursed soldiers' additional meanings. As one of its members explained, 'the accusation contained in the name cursed soldiers was addressed to the opinion-making elites of the early period of the Third Republic' (Fundacja Pamiętamy, 2009). The LR inscribed the notion of 'cursed soldiers' in the political struggle against the Third Republic (III RP), which it regarded as a system devoid of legitimacy and constituting a continuation of communism, which was to be proved by its politics of forgetting the PPP.

LR activists were driven by a moral feeling of resentment towards communists and post-communists who, in their view, occupied positions to which they had no moral right (Barbalet, 2004). As an LR member at the time recalled during an interview, 'cursed soldiers were inscribed on the banners of this radical part of the opposition (…) supporters of tough measures against the communist past (…) for me this was important in the 1990s, I had a sense of acute injustice'. The LR compared communists to Nazis and wanted to exclude them from public life, calling for them to be stripped of their voting rights. Referring to the symbolism of 'cursed soldiers' expressed their resentment and legitimised their radical anti-communism. 'Cursed soldiers' represented an uncompromising struggle against communism, presented in Manichean terms as an absolute evil to be opposed at all costs Liga Republikańska, 1993).

The LR framed itself as a grouping continuing the traditions of the 'cursed soldiers', thus legitimising its radical political programme and delegitimising the III RP as a system created as a result of a deal with the communists. The symbolism of 'cursed soldiers' became popular in various right-wing anti-communist circles. The notion's popularity in various nationalist circles was probably partly due to the fact that the term 'cursed' masked the fact that there were nationalists who cooperated with the communists in the PRL. The rhetoric of 'cursed soldiers' also fitted in with conspiracy theories about the Round Table as a communist secret service operation. The right framed itself as a continuation of the uncompromising 'cursed soldiers', contrasting itself with the treacherous liberal elite that made a secret agreement with the communists and enabled them to maintain their dominant position in the III RP. At the same time, this rhetoric was accompanied by a sense of moral rightness and superiority underpinned by selective references to the perfectionist ethics of Henryk Elzenberg and to the ethically committed poetry of Zbigniew Herbert (Wąsowski & Żebrowski, 1999). In this right-wing symbolic politics, 'cursed soldiers' were also surrounded by an aura of anti-establishment, which translated into the appeal of this symbolism among football ultras, who in Poland generally have far-right sympathies (Nosal et al., 2021). 'Cursed soldiers' thus found their way into football stadiums, becoming a symbol of ultras. Paradoxically, fans of football clubs that in the PRL were associated with the power ministries, such as Śląsk Wrocław (a former military sports club), led the way in displaying this symbolism. In the football context, this symbolism fitted in well with football fan violence, providing it with nationalist legitimacy.

The LR's rhetoric, however, cannot be taken for granted. After 1989, various ways of commemorating the anti-communist underground emerged, and it cannot be said that there was a deliberate politics of erasing them from collective memory. Free research on the underground began, families brought cases to the courts for the annulment of sentences and financial compensation, and veterans' organisations were formed and commemorated the partisans in various ways (Kurkowska-Budzan, 2009). In the Third Republic, PPP constituted an element of the mnemonic landscape, but it was not the central component of it. The state did not promote the commemoration of the PPP by means of any systematic memory politics, let alone by referring to the ideologically and emotionally charged symbolism of the 'cursed soldiers'. It can be said that the PPP was part of non-commemorative memory (Schudson, 1997). Specific figures were commemorated by focusing not so much on their anti-communist struggle but on the fact that they were victims of the communists in line with the dominant cosmopolitan memory regime, referring to universal human rights that were violated by totalitarian regimes (Ferrándiz & Hristova, 2021).

From the perspective of the dominant post-transformation memory politics after 1989, the symbolism of 'cursed soldiers' was unacceptable because it represented violence and radical anti-communism that equated the PRL with Nazi occupation. This symbolism contradicted the dominant mythology of democratic transformation, which proclaimed the praise of compromise as a great achievement of the democratic opposition and reformist communists that could serve as an example applicable worldwide giving hope for the peaceful resolution of conflicts (Pearce, 2015). The same was true, for example, in Spain during the democratic transition, where the aforementioned Maquis did not become central to memory politics because they did not fit into the dominant narrative of a peaceful transition to democracy (Gómez López-Quiñones & Moreno-Nuño, 2012). In Poland, the democratic transition was framed within a teleological vision of history, the goal of which was to be liberal democracy, a free market economy, and membership of the European Union. This process was presented as a unilinear and inevitable modernisation along the lines of Western European countries. Viewed in this light, the anti-communist underground appeared as an archaic violent movement at odds with Poland's modern aspirations and the European standards. Instead, hegemonic memory politics celebrated the Round Table, Solidarity and Lech Wałęsa as the icon of the Solidarity strikes, which was part of a wider trend of commemorating non-violent movements.

References

Babczenko, J., & Bolduan, R. (1969). *Front bez okopów [A front without trenches].* Gdańsk: Wydawnictwo Morskie.
Barbalet, J. M. (2004). *Emotion, social theory, and social structure: A macrosociological approach.* Cambridge: Cambridge University Press.
Bojko, Ł. (2020). *Rozstrzelane pokolenie [The executed generation].* Cracow: eSPe
Borodziej, W. (2006). *The Warsaw Uprising of 1944.* Madison: University of Wisconsin Press.
Chmielarz, A., Kunert, A. K., & Piontek, E. (2000). *Proces moskiewski przywódców Polskiego Państwa Podziemnego [The Moscow trial of the leaders of the Polish Underground State].* Warsaw: Rytm.
Connerton, P. (2008). Seven types of forgetting. *Memory Studies, 1*(1), 59–71.
Czykwin, E. (2011). Interpelacja nr 22124 do prezesa Rady Ministrów w sprawie wypłaty odszkodowań osobom pokrzywdzonym w wyniku działań grup zbrojnych w latach 1944–1956 [Parliamentary question No. 22124 to the Prime Minister on the payment of compensation to persons injured by armed groups in 1944–1956]. Retrieved from https://orka2.sejm.gov.pl/IZ6.nsf/main/7FD5603F
Ferrándiz, F., & Hristova, M. (2021). The production of memory modes during mass grave exhumations in contemporary Europe. In S. Berger, & W. Kansteiner (Eds.), *Agonistic memory and the legacy of 20th century wars in Europe* (pp. 39–67). Cham: Palgrave Macmillan.
Fundacja Pamiętamy. (2009). Z Grzegorzem Wąsowskim z Fundacji "Pamiętamy" rozmawia Jarosław Wróblewski [Grzegorz Wąsowski of the 'Pamiętamy' Foundation is interviewed by Jarosław Wróblewski]. Retrieved from https://www.fundacjapamietamy.pl/index.php?option=com_content&view=article&id=3&Itemid=64

Gehler, M., & Schrifft, D. (2020). *Violent resistance: From the Baltics to Central, Eastern and South Eastern Europe 1944–1956*. Paderborn: Brill.
Gómez López-Quiñones, A., & Moreno-Nuño, C. (Eds.). (2012). *Hispanic issues: Armed resistance: Cultural representations of the anti-Francoist guerrilla*. Minneapolis: Minnesota UP.
Grzymkowski, J. (1976). Rówieśnicy [The peers]. Warsaw: WRiT.
Hristova, M., & Żychlińska, M. (2020). Mass grave exhumations as patriotic retreat. *Human Remains and Violence, 6*(2), 42–60.
IPN. (2005). Informacja o ustaleniach końcowych śledztwa S 28/02/Zi w sprawie pozbawienia życia 79 osób – mieszkańców powiatu Bielsk Podlaski w tym 30 osób tzw. furmanów w lesie koło Puchał Starych, dokonanych w okresie od dnia 29 stycznia 1946r. do dnia 2 lutego 1946 [Information on final findings of investigation S 28/02/Zi on depriving 79 people of their lives – inhabitants of Bielsk Podlaski poviat, including 30 so-called carters in the forest near Puchały Stare, committed in the period from 29 January 1946 to 2 February 1946]. Retrieved from https://ipn.gov.pl/pl/dla-mediow/komunikaty/9989,Informacja-o-ustaleniach-koncowych-sledztwa-S-2802Zi-w-sprawie-pozbawienia-zycia.html
Jaskulowski, K., & Majewski, P. (2022). Populist in form, nationalist in content? Law and Justice, nationalism and memory politics. *European Politics and Society*. Advanced online publication. DOI: 10.1080/23745118.2022.2058752
Kochanski, H. (2012). *The eagle unbowed: Poland and the Poles in the Second World War*. Cambridge, MA: Harvard University Press. Kończal, K. (2020). The invention of the 'cursed soldiers' and its opponents: Post-war partisan struggle in contemporary Poland. *East European Politics and Societies, 34*(1), 67–95.
Kunicki, M. (2012). *Between the brown and the red: Nationalism, Catholicism, and communism in twentieth-century Poland: The politics of Boleslaw Piasecki*. Athens: Ohio University Press.
Kurkowska-Budzan, M. (2009). *Antykomunistyczne podziemie zbrojne na białostocczyźnie [Anticommunist armed underground in białystok area]*. Cracow: Towarzystwo Wydawnicze "Historia Iagiellonica".
Lesiakowski, K. (1998). *Mieczysław Moczar 'Mietek' [Mieczysław Moczar 'Mietek']*. Warsaw: Rytm.
Liga Republikańska. (1993). *Deklaracja Ligi Republikańskiej: Nasz Dzień Nadejdzie [Declaration of Liga Republikańska: Our day will come]*. Warsaw: Liga Republikańska.
Leszczyński, G. (2019). *Okręg Warszawski Zrzeszenia Wolność I Niezawisłość na tle struktur centralnych. [The Warsaw District of the Wolność I Niezawisłość Association in the context of central structures]*. Warsaw: Fundacja im. Jadwigi Chylińskiej.
Machejek, W. (1955/1965). *Rano przeszedł huragan [A hurricane passed through in the morning]*. Warsaw: MON.
Marco, J. (2016). *Guerrilleros and neighbours in arms: Identities and cultures of the anti-fascist resistance in Spain*. Brighton: Sussex Academic Press.
Mazur, M. (2019). *Antykomunistycznego podziemia portret zbiorowy 1945–1956 [A collective portrait of the anti-communist underground 1945–1956]*. Warsaw and Lublin: Bellona.
Nosal, P., Kossakowski, R., & Woźniak, W. (2021). Guerrilla patriotism and mnemonic wars: Cursed soldiers as role models for football fans in Poland. *Sport in Society, 24*(11), 2050–2065.
Osęka, P. (2008). *Marzec '68 [March '68]*. Cracow: Znak.

Paczkowski, A. (1994). *Stanisław Mikołajczyk*. Warsaw: WsiP.
Panz, K. (2015). 'Why did they, who had suffered so much and endured, have to die?' The Jewish victims of armed violence in Podhale (1945–1947). *Zagłada Żydów. Studia i Materiały, 11*, 33–89.
Pearce, S. C. (2015). Who owns a movement's memory? The case of Poland's solidarity. In A. Reading, & T. Katriel (Eds.), *Cultural memories of nonviolent struggles* (pp. 166–187). London: Palgrave Macmillan.
Polniak, Ł. (2011). *Patriotyzm wojskowy w PRL w latach 1956–1970 [Military patriotism in the PRL between 1956 and 1970]*. Warsaw: Wydawnictwo Trio.
Polniak, Ł. (2016). Trzy obrazy Żołnierzy Wyklętych w propagandzie kinowej PRL z lat 1960–1989 [Three images of cursed soldiers in the communist propaganda cinema in 1969–1989]. *Społeczeństwo i Ekonomia, 2*, 52–73.
Przetakiewicz, Z. (1994). *Od ONR-u do PAX-u [From ONR to PAX]*. Warsaw: KP.
Przetakiewicz, Z. M., et al. (2022). *Bolesław Piasecki: od wodza RNR "Falanga" do przewodniczącego Stowarzyszenia Pax i członka rady państwa PRL. [Bolesław Piasecki: from the leader of the "Falanga" RNR to the chairman of the Pax Association and member of the PRL State Council]*. Warsaw: Centrum Edukacji i Rozwoju im. Biskupa Kajetana Sołtyka.
Raina, P. (1994). *Kościół w PRL. Kościół katolicki a państwo w świetle dokumentów 1945–1989 [The Church in the PRL. The Catholic Church and the State in the light of documents 1945–1989]*. Poznań: W Drodze.
Schudson, M. (1997). Lives, laws, and language: Commemorative versus non-commemorative forms of effective public memory. *Communication Review, 2*(1), 3–18.
Ślaski, J. (1981). Przeklęci wykreśleni. Oni też byli polakami [Cursed and crossed out. They too were Poles]. *Słowo Powszechne, 218*(10706), 4.
Ślaski, J. (1996). *Żołnierze wyklęci [Cursed soldiers]*. Warsaw: Rytm.
Tokarska-Bakir, J. (2017). The Polish underground organization Wolność i Niezawisłość and anti-Jewish pogroms, 1945–6. *Patterns of Prejudice, 51*(2), 111–136.
Tomasik, W. (1994). Aparat bezpieczeństwa w literaturze polskiej okresu socrealizmu [The security apparatus in Polish literature of the socialist realist period]. *Pamiętnik Literacki, 85*, 73–85.
Wałach, S. (1971). *Był w Polsce czas... [There was a time in Poland]*. Wydawnictwo Literackie.
Wąsowski, G., & Żebrowski, L. (1999). *Żołnierze Wyklęci: Antykomunistyczne podziemie zbrojne po 1944 roku [Cursed Soldiers: The anti-communist armed underground after 1944]*. Warsaw: Volumen.
Wnuk, R. (2020). Armed anti-Communist resistance in Poland, 1944–1956. In M. Gehler, & D. Schriffl (Eds.), *Violent resistance: From the Baltics to Central, Eastern and South Eastern Europe 1944–1956* (pp. 90–121). Paderborn: Brill.
Zaremba, M. (2006). *Communism – Legitimacy – Nationalism*. Frankfurt am Main: Peter Lang.

4 Building Hegemony
The Memory Politics of Cursed Soldiers

Takeover

In the 1990s, right-wing memorial activism focused on the symbolism of 'cursed soldiers' functioned on the margins of public life. There were various initiatives commemorating members of the PPP, but these concerned specific organisations and figures. The very notion of 'cursed soldiers' appeared mainly in the right-wing press and books. Right-wing memorial activists later stated with exaggeration that the commemoration of the PPP was a 'hobbyist fringe', confusing commemorations of the PPP with references to the ideologically loaded symbolism of 'cursed soldiers' (Arseniuk & Musiał, 2015, p. 315). However, since the early 2000s, the symbolism of 'cursed soldiers' has been gradually incorporated into mainstream politics (Kończal, 2020). The symbol was gradually appropriated by PiS, which preached the need for radical moral renewal (Jaskulowski & Kilias, 2016). PiS framed the III RP as a socially unjust system marginalising the economically underprivileged. At the same time, PiS portrayed this system as nationally alienated, ruled by liberal elites pursuing foreign interests (Jaskulowski & Majewski, 2022). In the PiS rhetoric, social marginalisation was linked to the anti-national character of the III RP, since it was in the interests of foreign countries that Poles should constitute a poor labour force that foreign capital could employ in assembly plants erected on Polish territory. PiS proclaimed the need to replace the elite with a truly national vanguard that would govern in accordance with the interests of all Poles, not just a narrow privileged group (Bill, 2022). In this context, PiS used the symbolism of the 'cursed soldiers' to frame itself as an anti-establishment party leading the fight against the socially unjust and anti-national system (Jaskulowski & Majewski, 2022).

Incorporating the symbolism of 'cursed soldiers' into mainstream politics met with little resistance from other parties. The most decisive resistance originated in a left-wing circle centred around the magazine *Tygodnik Przegląd*, involved the Belarusian minority, and included some historians. *Tygodnik Przegląd*, for example, promoted the publication of a series of books under the slogan 'wyklęci nie święci' (cursed are not saints), which described

DOI: 10.4324/9781003368847-4
This chapter has been made available under a CC-BY-NC-ND 4.0 license.

various crimes of the PPP and also called on the left to create its own memory politics (Dybicz & Woroncow, 2019). Belarusian activists also protested against the commemoration of partisans who had committed crimes, e.g. by filing various parliamentary questions in the Sejm, but their voice was marginalised. Some historians also spoke out critically but nevertheless had little influence on the development of the 'cursed soldiers' memory politics, and were subjected to various harassments when PiS took power (Leszczyński, 2020; Poleszak, 2020; Radio Maryja, 2020).

Paradoxically, the centre-right parties, namely the Civic Platform (PO) and the Polish People's Party (PSL), helped in this incorporation, although this symbolism delegitimised these parties. Indeed, the right-wing narrative undermined the right of these parties to speak on behalf of the Polish nation. It accused leading politicians of these parties of having participated in the 'conspiracy' at the Round Table and of having co-created the post-communist III RP (Jaskulowski, 2012; Żuk & Żuk, 2018). Right-wing rhetoric evoked a vision of building a new state and society breaking with the previous system, providing cover for the rule of communist security agents. PiS framed itself as the only party being the heir to the 'cursed soldiers' (Jaskulowski & Majewski, 2022). Two issues were crucial in the incorporation process, namely the activities of the IPN and the inclusion of the symbolism of 'cursed soldiers' in the calendar of national official days (Kończal, 2020).

With regard to the IPN, 2005 was a key year, when Janusz Kurtyka (2005–2010) became president of this institution with the support of right-centre parties (Kończal, 2020). Kurtyka was politically affiliated with various conservative and Catholic organisations; he was also the editor of a magazine dedicated to WiN, as well as the president of the WiN veteran association. He believed that the post-war underground was one of the most momentous developments in Poland's recent history (Arseniuk & Musiał, 2015; Kuta & Tęsiorowski, 2019). He greatly overestimated its scale, claiming that up to 500,000 people may have belonged to the underground (Mazur, 2022, p. 432). Kurtyka supported the use of the ideologically and emotionally charged term 'cursed soldiers' in line with right-wing rhetoric. At the same time, he portrayed himself as an objective researcher. He claimed that anti-communist partisans were Polish national heroes of whom every Pole should be proud, formulating a kind of emotional criterion of national belonging. Consequently, 'cursed soldiers' were to be at the centre of the state's memory politics. As Kurtyka said in his missionary fervour after taking over as IPN president, 'we are like the Jews after their escape from Egyptian slavery, wandering in the desert for 40 years waiting (...) for leaders (...) who will lead the nation into the Promised Land' (Arseniuk & Musiał, 2015, p. 512).

Under the leadership of Kurtyka, the IPN began to engage more vigorously in the commemoration of 'cursed soldiers' and in undermining the existing key memorial symbols. In 2008, the IPN published a comprehensive book on Lech Walesa (Cenckiewicz & Gontarczyk, 2008). This was the first book on

Wałęsa published by the IPN and, characteristically, it analysed exclusively the alleged secret agent collaboration of the Solidarity leader with the Security Service (Dmochowska, 2008; Friszke, 2008). Even though Kurtyka appeared to disengage with such interpretations, the book still fit within and gave credibility to the right-wing narrative. This narrative suggests the Round Table and the post-1989 political transformation were parts of a communist conspiracy, presenting 'scientific evidence' upheld by the authority of the official memory politics institution.

At the same time, the IPN started to put more emphasis on developing research, education, popularisation, and commemorative activities centred on 'cursed soldiers'. It is difficult to separate these activities from each other, as behind all of them, including research, was the conviction that cursed soldiers are national heroic figures who should be honoured. Research on the PPP was presented in terms of a national duty as restoring the memory of national heroes. Exhumation sites were described in terms of the national sacrum as places sanctified by the blood of national martyrs, whose remains were treated as sacred things (Hristova & Żychlińska, 2020). As, for example, the historian in charge of the exhumation work reverently said of the found personal belongings of the partisans shown in the museum exhibition, 'we are presenting relics of cursed soldiers' (Ministerstwo Sprawiedliwości, 2018). The IPN engaged in activities aimed at the general public, for example, by organising open-air exhibitions in main streets or squares. Such exhibitions presented 'cursed soldiers' and security service officers. As was explained, preserving the memory of the victims also raises the question of the identity of the perpetrators, who cannot remain anonymous. For example, in 2006, an exhibition entitled 'Faces of the Wrocław Security Service' was opened on the market square in Wrocław, displaying photographs, names, and biographies of employees of local branches of the Security Service. The biographies provided information on the so-called 'proper names' of the officers, a pretext to demonstrate that some officers had surnames commonly associated with Jews (IPN, 2006). Pictorial photographs of the corpses of partisans killed in battle or murdered by the communists became an element of similar exhibitions. This politics of the macabre is intended to illustrate the cruelty of the communists and to reinforce the image of the 'cursed soldiers' as innocent victims (no mention was made of PPP victims).

Other forms of the IPN's popularisation activities included feature and documentary film promotions, preparation of special supplements to various newspapers and magazines, meetings with journalists, events with book authors, concerts, motorbike rallies, and runs. The IPN has also begun to attach importance to involving young people and children in the commemoration of 'cursed soldiers', which is achieved by promoting books that present the partisans' life as an idealistic adventure in an attractive way. One example is the promotion of a book for children aged 10 entitled *Knights of the Forest*. The book portrays partisans as righteous and honourable people; it does not talk about the atrocities of war but presents it in the convention of a play in which children can easily engage (Gajewska & Zaguła, 2013). Other IPN activities include various essay or poem competitions, sports events or urban games organised in cooperation with schools, and various right-wing organisations and private companies (e.g. selling 'patriotic' clothing). The IPN also works closely with the aforementioned We Remember Foundation, whose activists have participated in various events organised by the IPN, such as lectures or conferences, thereby contributing to the popularisation of the term 'cursed soldiers', which was also supported by the Association of Soldiers of the National Armed Forces (IK, 2014). IPN employees started to take part in the rituals of unveiling monuments and plaques commemorating cursed soldiers. The pattern of such ritual commemorations, which take place in a national-religious-military scenography, has since become established (Alexander, 2006). Typical commemorations include the consecration of a monument/plaque by a local Catholic priest and a mass attended by representatives of local authorities, the military, and IPN staff. During the mass, IPN historians tell the story of the commemorated partisans according to the hagiographical convention and hand out IPN publications, and the mass is followed by a roll call of the fallen (Koń--czal, 2020).

Another important element was the inclusion of the commemoration of the PPP in the official calendar of national days. This process was gradual and its first heralds were the Sejm resolutions commemorating the PPP. The first resolution was passed by the Sejm in 2001 honouring WiN. The Democratic Left Alliance (Sojusz Lewicy Demokratycznej, SLD) MPs spoke against the resolution, arguing that WiN members had committed crimes. Right-wing and centrist MPs either denied the crimes or marginalised them. Interestingly, in the discussion, only a single right-wing MP used the term 'cursed soldiers', showing that the phrase had not entered mainstream political vocabulary (Sejm, 2001). The next step was the adoption by the PiS-dominated Sejm in 2006 of a resolution already referring to the concept of 'cursed soldiers', symbolised in the document by Zygmunt Szendzielarz 'Łupaszka'. Thus, one can hardly agree with Końćzal that it was only after 2015 that memory politics became radicalised, when the NSZ also began to be included among cursed soldiers. Łupaszka was not a member of the NSZ but historians indicate that he was responsible for war crimes – his unit murdered the Lithuanian and Belarusian population (Dybicz & Woroncow, 2019; Rokicki, 2015). In the communicative memory of the Belarusian minority, Łupaszka functions as a criminal. In fact, a Belarusian MP spoke against the bill, but his voice was ignored and all parties except the SLD voted in favour of the resolution (Sejm, 2006).

Various veteran groups and right-wing activists campaigned for the establishment of a new national day. These plans were supported by the PiS-linked President Lech Kaczyński, who in 2009, for example, wrote in a letter to the participants of one of the commemorations that restoring the memory of the 'cursed soldiers' was important task of his presidency. The letter ended with the words 'Honour the memory of the soldiers of the National Armed Forces'

(Kaczyński, 2009). In 2009, veterans' organisations and the Opole authorities made an appeal to MPs to establish 1 March as a public holiday. The campaign was coordinated by Opole's vice-president Arkadiusz Karbowiak, who belonged to the PO but was also active in extreme right-wing and neo-fascist milieus (after PiS won the elections, Karbowiak supervised the construction of a museum of the 'cursed soldiers' on Rakowiecka Street in Warsaw). Karbowiak wrote in the far-right press about 'so-called Nazi war crimes' (Pankowski, 2010). The appeal was addressed to all parties except the SLD because, as Karbowiak explained, 'this party is alien to the independence tradition' (Ambroziak, 2009).

The initiative was supported by the PO and PiS parliamentary groups, as well as by President Kaczyński, who took the legislative initiative and drafted the bill. The presidential bill spoke directly about the 'anti-communist uprising' and proposed establishing a national day for 'cursed soldiers' (Kończal, 2020). The legislative work was interrupted by Kaczyński's death in a plane crash at Smolensk in April 2010. Some right-wing politicians began to suggest immediately after the crash that the Russian special services were behind the accident. In time, a conspiracy theory emerged that Putin had colluded with Tusk to assassinate the president in order to get rid of an obstructive politician (Aleszumm, 2014; Jaskulowski, 2012). Bronisław Komorowski, who became president after the catastrophe, continued to work on establishing a new holiday. At the beginning of 2011, the Sejm passed a law stating that 1 March would be the National Day of Remembrance of Cursed Soldiers. The law no longer referred to an 'uprising' but idealised the partisans as 'heroes' fighting to defend 'independence' and the 'democratic aspirations of Polish society'. The act was presented as an element of President Kaczyński's political testament, thus creating a kind of atmosphere of moral blackmail, which probably influenced all parties to support the act, including the SLD (Sejm, 2011, 2012).

After winning the 2015 elections, PiS elevated 'cursed soldiers' to the status of a key symbol of its memory politics. The party took over and monopolised the symbol of 'cursed soldiers', presenting itself as the only legitimate heir of the PPP, guarantor of Polish independence and guardian of national interests. Thus, there was a further institutionalisation that involved several processes. State ceremonies associated with the celebration of 'cursed soldiers' acquired greater significance and stature. The scale, including the financial involvement of the state, the Catholic Church, as well as various NGOs, foundations, veterans' organisations, and the IPN, increased. Admittedly, this tendency was already visible before, but now it has become more pronounced, and the ritual of celebrating the day of 'cursed soldiers' has acquired an unambiguously nationalistic, Catholic, and militaristic dimension. The presence of the highest Catholic Church hierarchs, bishops or archbishops, and the highest representatives of the authorities – the president, prime minister, ministers, voivodes, the army, and representatives of various institutions of memory politics – has become a regular feature of the celebrations (Jaskulowski & Majewski, 2022).

For example, in 2020, President Andrzej Duda participated in the 'Tracing the Wolf' run. In the afternoon at the Presidential Palace, he presented state honours to the still living anti-communist partisans and then took part in the central ceremonies that took place in front of the Tomb of the Unknown Soldier in Józef Piłsudski Square in Warsaw, a highly symbolically and emotionally charged place. The ceremonies were attended by representatives of the government, the Catholic Church, and the military. During the ceremony, the roll call of the fallen was read out, and the President, who is the supreme head of the armed forces, awarded general promotions of the Polish army and took the military oath from 2,000 soldiers. He gave a speech setting out 'cursed soldiers' as a model of sacrifice for the fatherland. Central rituals often last all day and also include ceremonies in front of the Pantheon of Cursed soldiers at 'Łączka' in Powązki Military Cemetery (the Pantheon was built while the PO-PSL government was still in power, which ceremonially unveiled it in 2015), in front of a commemorative plaque in the former Detention Centre of the Public Security Office on Rakowiecka Street (now a museum). Politicians also visit other sites related to the history of the underground, especially the places where they were imprisoned and murdered, where they lay flowers. The commemorations are accompanied by masses for the intention of the soldiers and a number of other events such as film screenings, lectures, exhibitions, concerts, conferences, workshops for children, historical re-enactments, etc.

The ritual of celebrating the day of the 'cursed soldiers' takes place in a nationalist, Catholic, and military scenography saturated with thick and emotional symbolism referring to Polish history (Alexander, 2006). This symbolism evokes in a condensed way the whole mythical-symbolic complex referring to national martyrdom, creating an emotional atmosphere of sadness and suffering. As a participant in such celebrations explains, 'here it is more like commemorating their deaths (…) at the marches it is actually, especially here after all, the night one. Well it's in silence, it's with candles and torches, and… you know, it's commemorating their deaths'. At the same time, however, the ritual glorifies the heroism of the partisans and constructs their struggle as tragic but ultimately victorious. During the various speeches, the metaphor of the land fertilised by the bloodshed and the image of the seed yielding a new crop in the form of new generations of patriots continuing the mission of the 'cursed soldiers' is often evoked (Čolović, 2002). Thus, the ritual is not exhausted by the bloody and sacrifice metaphors, as it is accompanied by a number of other events that also create an atmosphere of pride in the bravery, heroism, and stamina of the 'cursed soldiers' and the joy of the far-reaching victorious results of their struggle, i.e. the final collapse of communism. As the participant says:

> I think there's a double kind of… I think it's a bit ambiguous here. Because on the one hand, yes, let's assume on the night we celebrate their death, but on the other hand… for example some kind of raid, that we commemorate

them, that they fought, didn't they? And there is a joy of victory I would say, over communism, over this partitioning power. So it's kind of you know, two in one. I think, I think, I don't mind if I would, for example, go at night and commemorate their memory and then I would, for example, during the day their heroic deeds.

The interviewee emphasises the value of armed struggle and frames the struggle of the 'cursed soldiers' as victorious, in line with the hegemonic discourse. He also externalises communism by equating it to the partitioning powers, i.e. something external to Poland, which also reflects the dominant discourse. He de-historicises the struggle of the 'cursed soldiers' by constructing it as another national uprising (a struggle against the partitioner), a kind of eternal return of the same struggle of Poles for independence.

Similar ceremonies are held at the local level; for example, in Lublin in 2022 the celebrations started with the governor laying flowers at the Monument to those murdered in Lublin Castle between 1944 and 1954. Flowers were also laid at the monument to 'cursed soldiers' at St Michael the Archangel Church, at the NSZ monument on the NSZ roundabout and at the WiN monument on the WiN roundabout. At noon, a mass for the intention of 'cursed soldiers' was held at the Holy Family Church at 11 Jan Paweł II Street. It was followed by a lecture by a historian from the Catholic University of Lublin who warned against gender ideology and argued that the tradition of 'cursed soldiers' obliges us to work against this neo-Marxist doctrine, which threatens Polish families. In the evening, the Memorial March of Cursed Soldiers passed through Lublin, which was dominated by fascist nationalists chanting 'Honour and glory to the heroes'. The march ended with the NSZ prayer that was recited in the partisan units, which among other things states: 'Let from the blood of our innocently shed brothers (...) a Great Poland be created'. Since 2015, fascist nationalists have also organised a provocative march in Hajnówka in honour of Bury, in the largely Belarusian-populated area where his unit was active. In 2022, for example, a group of about a hundred people marched through the town, chanting 'Bury, Bury our hero', 'Death to the enemies of the fatherland', carrying anti-Semitic banners evoking the myth of Judeo-Communism, to the music of a neo-Nazi band. Paradoxically, the marchers also chanted the name of Pilecki, who is a symbol of Poles helping Jews. This relatively small march has attracted media attention due to protests by local residents and left-wing MPs trying to recall the crimes of 'Bury' against the Belarusian population. However, after PiS took power, official memory institutions denied the partisan's crimes, the IPN rejected the findings of its own earlier investigation and promoted Bury as a national hero, and the IPN president defended Bury, saying he 'brutalised the forms of struggle against the terrifying enemy of the fatherland' (IPN, 2019; PAP, 2021).

After 2015, the scale of the state's involvement in memory politics increased significantly, which translated into a high increase in funding for

IPN activities. PiS has also created a variety of new memory politics institutions, such as the Roman Dmowski and Ignacy Jan Paderewski Institute for the Heritage of National Thought and the Witold Pilecki Institute of Solidarity and Valour. The former deals with the history and commemoration of the ethnic-authoritarian and fascist nationalist movement, including the NSZ. The latter aims to commemorate Poles who helped other Polish citizens between 1917 and 1990. In fact, the institute concentrates on commemorating Poles who helped Jews, constituting an imitation of Yad Vashem, allowing it to bypass its criteria (Kowalska-Leder, 2023). Characteristically, the institute is named after Witold Pilecki, who has a double function in hegemonic politics: he is an iconic representation of 'cursed soldiers' and also of Poles helping Jews. It should be added that another 'Polish Yad Vashem' is being constructed next to the St John Paul II Museum of Memory and Identity in Toruń, built by Tadeusz Rydzyk (Catholic priest and religious who created a conservative-nationalist media-education conglomerate) with state aid. As we will continue to explain, the memory politics of 'cursed soldiers' is linked in various ways to the issue of Polish-Jewish relations, being a manifestation of the rivalry of suffering. PiS has also established specialised museums dedicated to the PPP: the Museum of Cursed Soldiers and Political Prisoners of the Polish People's Republic on Rakowiecka Street in Warsaw and the Museum of Cursed Soldiers in Ostrołęka. The involvement of state-owned companies, which, for example, finance the International Film Festival NNV devoted to the PPP, has also increased.

PiS also reorganised the school system in 2017, which it used to revise the history core curriculum. In 2022, it introduced an additional class on recent political past, History and the Present. According to PiS, history education was in the crisis caused by its alleged cosmopolitan focus and emphasis on learning historical methods rather than strengthening students' national identity. Although PiS framed its reforms as radical changes, it actually reinforced the already dominant nationalist model of history education, i.e. the tendency to subordinate history teaching to ideological goals, namely cultivation of the belief that the nation is the highest moral value (Jaskulowski & Majewski, 2020; Jaskulowski & Surmiak, 2017; Jaskulowski et al., 2018, 2022). PiS's changes to history education strengthened the position of those teachers who defined history teaching in terms of a Polish-centric history designed to generate pride and loyalty to the achievements of a patriarchal and closed Polish nation (MEN, 2018). 'Cursed soldiers' occupy a key place in modified history education. For example, the core curriculum for the subject History and the Present promotes a right-wing narrative about the anti-communist uprising in post-war Poland. It presents 'cursed soldiers' as 'an example of allegiance to principles and bravery' and as moral role models (IPN, 2021; MEN, 2022, n.d.). Schools also organise the commemorations of the national day of 'cursed soldiers'. On this occasion, plays, choir performances, poetry recitations, and competitions are presented. The life of the various partisans is recalled, and they are cherished in an elevated quasi-religious convention: 'Her [Inka's] immaculate, almost saintly figure has a special unifying power for many Poles and the testimony of her life is the cause of the spiritual rebirth of many people' (Gałka, 2013).

Symbolic Thickening

Simultaneously with institutionalisation, PiS, in the process of symbolic thickening, assigned a number of meanings to the symbol of 'cursed soldiers' in line with its ideology (Kotwas & Kubik, 2019). The simple symbol of anti-communism underwent a multidimensional process of signifying thickening, which consisted of several elements: nationalisation, sacralisation, Catholicisation, ethnicisation, Europeanisation, masculinisation, moralisation, and further radicalisation (Jaskulowski & Majewski, 2023). Thus, in the process of nationalisation, 'cursed soldiers' began to represent more clearly the struggle for a Polish sovereign nation-state. Hegemonic memory politics inscribed the 'cursed soldiers' into the history of Polish national liberation struggles as another national uprising lasting from 1944 to 1963 (the militia then shot the last 'partisan'). The post-war partisans are depicted as another incarnation of the age-old struggle of Poles to maintain or regain their independence and, in defence of the values of Latin civilisation, a new embodiment of the same struggle against various powers – the Kościuszko Uprising, the November Uprising, and the January Uprising.

The symbol of 'cursed soldiers' has also become sacralised. Memory politics frames the partisans as national heroes sacrificing their lives for the nation, elevating them to a symbol to be revered and cherished. Referring to Durkheim's categories, it can be said that memory politics gives cursed soldiers the status of a sacrum, i.e. a thing excluded from everyday life and surrounded by respect, because it represents Polish national values and is intended to perform integrative functions, providing a symbolic glue for national unity (Durkheim, 1912/2008). The rhetoric of shedding/sacrificing blood and lives for the nation further reinforces the sacred nature of the symbol by framing the 'cursed soldiers' as martyrs who died for the nation. This language of the secular sacrum is compounded by the association of 'cursed soldiers' with Catholicism, which, as we have seen, is defined as the basis of Polish national identity by PiS. One of the main symbols of 'cursed soldiers' has become a gorget with the Virgin Mary. On the one hand, this is a reference to the nationalist-religious notion that Poland is a chosen nation under the special protection of the Mother of God (Niedźwiedź, 2005). On the other hand, it elevates the male partisan community by depicting them as defenders of the faith and the nation personified by the figure of a mother who is a model of femininity. As we have also written, ceremonies commemorating cursed soldiers are also attended by the hierarchy of the Catholic Church, who emphasise the intrinsic link between Polishness and Catholicism. In this way, the Catholic clergy reinforce the sacral nature of this symbol by giving it a transcendental dimension, which is another manifestation of the melding of nationalism and Catholicism (Jaskulowski, 2012). A vivid illustration of this fusion in the context of 'cursed soldiers' is the popular slogan chanted during various commemorative demonstrations and rallies: 'Inka is looking down on us from heaven, she behaved as she should'. Death for the fatherland is framed here as ensuring immortality in a twofold sense: Inka will live forever in the national collective memory, and she has also achieved salvation in the Catholic sense.

The symbol of the 'cursed soldiers' also underwent a process of ethnicisation, i.e. it became a symbol of Polishness understood in terms of exclusionary criteria of national belonging in line with the stereotype of the (white) Pole-Catholic. This memory politics also set emotional criteria of Polishness, implying that whoever does not feel pride in the achievements of partisans and respect for this memorial symbol cannot really be Polish. Paradoxically, there was also a Europeanisation of this symbol, i.e. it came to represent the defence of European civilisation – in the imagination of authoritarian nationalism, Poland not only belongs to Europe but is its spiritual centre (Brubaker, 2017). In the right-wing rhetoric, Poland is the only country that cherishes Christian traditions and the values of classical Greek and Roman cultures, which are the foundations of genuine European civilisation. Poland also has exceptional merits in defending European civilisation against various external enemies, acting as a kind of rotating bulwark and repelling attacks: Turks, Russians, communists or, more recently, Muslim refugees. In this context, the symbolism of the 'cursed soldiers' emphasises the fight against communism defined as alien to European civilisation and the Polish nation. Defining the PRL as a foreign totalitarian state erases it from Polish national history as something external to it. This precludes any comparison of the PRL with the socially and nationally exclusionary Sanacja dictatorship of 1926–1939 (e.g. there are structural similarities between the cult of Józef Piłsudski in the Second Republic and Bolesław Bierut in the PRL or comparable patterns of state violence against social protest in both political systems).

Memory politics defines communism in civilisational terms as the creation of an alien and barbaric Eastern civilisation. The defence of this civilisation is a task for men, women only play an auxiliary role here (like Inka, who was a nurse and a courier) – we also have here a process of masculinisation, i.e. 'cursed soldiers' have become a symbol of patriarchal masculinity and a clear division of social sex roles, which is threatened, according to right-wing rhetoric, by Western 'gender' ideology. The promoters of 'gender' ideology seek to destroy 'traditional' family, which is the basis for the existence of the Polish nation and Christian European civilisation (Bratcher, 2020). 'Cursed soldiers' have also become, in the process of moralisation, the embodiment of ethical principles whose foundation is loyalty and sacrifice for the nation. In line with nationalist ideology, memory politics assumes that there is no morality without the nation, or to paraphrase a line attributed to Fyodor Dostoevsky: if there is no attachment to the nation, then everything is allowed. Let us recall again the nurse Inka, whom memory politics has elevated to the iconic representation of 'cursed soldiers'. It is claimed that Inka, while awaiting execution in prison, said to pass on that she had behaved as she should. This example embodies the heroic attitude of sacrificing one's life for the nation set as a model of moral excellence. At the same time, however, hegemonic politics extols a willingness not only to die for the nation but also to kill in the name of the nation, which manifests itself in a further radicalisation of memory politics that glorifies partisans such as the aforementioned Romuald Rajs 'Bury'. Despite the fact that the IPN found Bury responsible for genocide, he was included in the pantheon of national heroes, and monuments are erected to him (Boguszewski, 2017).

As a result, the symbol of the 'cursed soldiers' has become laden with a whole network of additional ideological meanings. PiS has transformed 'cursed soldiers' into a meaningfully and emotionally complex symbol that represents in a condensed way the right-wing understanding of the Polish nation. 'Cursed soldiers' have become a key memorial symbol of hegemonic memory politics that functions according to the logic of the summarising symbol (Ortner, 1973). According to this logic, the meanings of this symbolism are linked to each other on the principle of 'all or nothing'. The symbol of the 'cursed soldiers' represents a right-wing mythical-symbolic complex that constitutes a conglomerate of ideas, emotions and meanings, must be either accepted in their entirety or rejected, thus placing oneself outside the Polish nation. As one employee of a memory institution put it, the attitude towards 'cursed soldiers' is a 'litmus test', indicating which values someone believes in and which they reject. Thus, the symbol of the 'cursed soldiers' is a tangible and concrete embodiment of national identity and national symbolic boundaries (the Polish nation as 'cursed soldiers'). It delineates the boundary between us true Poles (anti-communists, Catholics, traditionalists, right-wingers, etc.) who support PiS, the only heir to the tradition of the struggle for independence, and all the rest of the internal enemies (Marxists, liberals, leftists, communists, etc.) who need to be re-educated and restored to the nation, and represents the boundaries that separate us Poles from the various external enemies against whom Poland needs to be defended.

Cursed Soldiers, Anti-Semitism and 'Others'

As part of the symbolic thickening, it is also necessary to consider the interconnection between the symbolism of 'cursed soldiers' and anti-Semitism, which at first glance may not be clear. However, the takeover of the symbolism of 'cursed soldiers' by PiS did not occur at an accidental time (Jaskulowski & Majewski, 2023). An important context for this politics was the debate about the involvement of some Poles in the Holocaust that was sparked by Jan

Tomasz Gross's book *Neighbours* (2001), describing how Poles murdered Jews in Jedwabne in 1941. Gross's subsequent books such as *Fear* (2006) and other studies showing that some Poles were murdered during the Second World War and after the war provoked angry reactions from the right (Grabowski, 2013). After PiS took power in 2015, it attempted to criminally restrict the freedom of research into Poles' involvement in the Holocaust. Although PiS withdrew the sanction of a prison sentence, it is possible to bring a civil suit against a researcher for imputing Nazi crimes to the Polish nation (Dobrosielski, 2017; Hackmann, 2018).

The portrayal of Poles as perpetrators undermined the myth of the Polish nation as a victim, an important element of the right-wing ideology of Polish national identity (Porter-Szűcs, 2014). Polish nationalism (like many other Central-Eastern European nationalisms) is characterised by an emphasis on exceptional Polish suffering, which, in the context of the Second World War, translates into a competition over who was the greatest victim of that war and envy of the Holocaust (Katz, 2016; Subotic, 2019). According to the right wing nationalists, a claim that some Poles took part in the Holocaust is an unfounded accusation seeking to diminish the suffering of Poles. It is a manifestation – as one of our interviewees said – of the 'monopolisation of the Holocaust' by Jews who focus exclusively on their own suffering, position themselves as the only victims of the Second World War and accuse everyone of anti-Semitism and participation in the Holocaust in order to extort financial reparations for themselves.

This competition for suffering in the context of the Holocaust had already been initiated by the communists, who, as we have already written, resorted to nationalist rhetoric in order to increase their legitimacy (Kucia, 2019; Steinlauf, 1997; Walicki, 1994; Zaremba, 2006). Paradoxically, the right wing emphasises its radical anti-communism in memory politics, but at the same time it has taken over from the communists the mythology of martyrdom and the rhetoric of competition for suffering. The right wing not only promotes a vision of the Polish nation as the main victim of the Second World War but also emphasises that it was still a victim long after the war (Jaskulowski & Majewski, 2023). It emphasises the equivalence of the suffering of Poles and Jew and suggests that the Germans targeted the total annihilation of the Poles simply because they were Poles, and therefore pursued a similar extermination strategy towards the Poles as towards the Jews. Moreover, prominent officials responsible for memory politics belittled the suffering of the Jews, as exemplified by an article by Tomasz Panfil, then director of the Office of National Education of the local branch of the IPN. Panfil (2017) wrote that initially, during the German occupation, Jews were better off than Poles because the former had their own self-government in the ghettos, while the latter were deprived of it and were mass murdered. It should be added that Panfil had links with neo-fascist groups and became famous as a judicial expert by declaring that the combination of the Polish emblem with the Celtic cross and the slogan 'White Power' was 'awkward' but expressed patriotic intentions. Panfil is just one of many new IPN employees who have had links with neo-fascists. At the same time, since PiS took control of the IPN, historians whose research does not fit in with official memory politics have been dismissed (Jaskulowski & Majewski, 2023).

Equating the suffering of Poles and Jews is accompanied by claiming that crimes against Poles are diminished or ignored because the topic of suffering in the Second World War has been monopolised by Jews. These claims sometimes take the form of accusations that an attempt is being made to frame Poles as perpetrators of the Holocaust, which was also highlighted by many of the right-wing interviewees involved in memory politics. For example, right-wing memory politics treats misplaced phrase of 'Polish camps' appearing in the media as a manifestation of an organised international campaign against Poland, behind which Germany and the Jews stand. The Germans want in this way to shift the responsibility for the Holocaust onto the Poles and to clear themselves of guilt, while the Jews with such accusations prepare the ground for making financial claims against Poland. At the same time, memory politics denies the anti-Semitic crimes of Poles against Jews, framing such claims as another element in the international campaign to vilify Poland. Another strategy is to deny the anti-Semitic nature of the crimes by treating them as common crimes of which anyone could have been a victim, or by symbolically excluding the perpetrators from the Polish nation as national renegades not representing true Polishness (Dobrosielski, 2017). Official memory politics emphasises that Poles helped Jews en masse, even though, unlike in other occupied countries, this was punishable by death. A regular point is to highlight that Poles are the most numerous among the righteous among the nations of the world (but relative figures are never given, for example, in relation to the number of Jews in each country). As we have seen, Polish substitutes of sorts for Yad Vashem are also being created, such as the Pilecki Institute. One of the main areas of the institute's activity is the campaign to commemorate Poles who helped Jews, which is mainly focused on the areas around the death camp in Treblinka (eastern Mazovia). In fact, the area around the Treblinka camp was the site of the killing and robbing of Jews who escaped from transports to the camp by the local Polish population (Engelking & Grabowski, 2018). In this way, as historian Jan Grabowski has argued, the institute 'neutralises' the memory of Jewish suffering and instrumentalises the Holocaust for the purposes of Polish nationalist memory politics (Grabowski, 2021).

In the context of emphasising the uniqueness of the suffering of Poles, one can also consider the discourse of two totalitarianisms evoked by Polish hegemonic memory politics. This discourse is not something specific to Poland, as many other Eastern European nationalisms also refer to it by placing Nazism and communism on an equal footing. This discourse is sometimes used to justify collaboration with the Third Reich as a lesser evil than communism, which is also evident in Poland. For example, in 2018, during a visit to Germany, Prime Minister Mateusz Mazowiecki laid flowers on the graves of the aforementioned Holy Cross Mountains Brigade, which collaborated with the Nazis at the end of the war (Kończal, 2020).

It should be recalled here that traditionally Polish authoritarian nationalism tended to externalise communism as an ideology alien to Poles and associated with barbarian Eastern civilisation represented by various nationalities, especially Jews (Dobrosielski, 2017). Even today, right-wing publicists and historians reproduce such stereotypes. For example, as we read in a popular book, 'the national minorities of the Second Republic were generally indifferent or hostile to the idea of Polish independence, as a result of which they did not identify with Polishness and this was one of the reasons why they became involved in the communist movement' (Bojko, 2020, p. 58). And the communist movement in Poland itself was 'composed of an international band of villains – native traitors, denationalised Poles dragged from Russia, Jews, Russians, Ukrainians and Belorusians' (Bojko, 2020, p. 60). IPN historians reproduce the stereotype of Judeo-communism, meticulously counting people of Jewish origin among Polish communists, assuming that a Jew, even if they become a communist, will always be a Jew (in contrast to Poles who, by becoming communists, cease to be Poles). This tendency to externalise and nationalise communism was also evident in interviews with various memory activists, who generally emphasised the 'Russianness' and 'Easternness' of communism. They reproduced, as an example of *longue durée* cultural structures, the popular notion in the interwar period that Russia was an Eastern Asiatic barbarian civilisation that provided fertile ground for communism. As one interviewee said of the Russians troops entering Poland in 1944, 'they wore ten watches, the hell they drank from the toilet... Well, because it's true, isn't it? Scum, scum, it was scum'.

This discourse of the two totalitarianisms is inscribed in the emphasis on the exceptional martyrdom of the Poles, as it not only allows for emphasising the equivalence of the suffering of Poles and Jews but guarantees the victory of the former in the competition of who suffered more. Moreover, this discourse also includes the suggestion, sometimes expressed explicitly, that Jews and other national minorities are responsible for the persecution of Poles under communism. Thus, hegemonic memory politics suggests that while Jews were victims of Nazi Germany alone, Poles were persecuted by the Third Reich as well as the Soviet, the PRL and national minorities. The dominant discourse emphasises not only the mass nature and cruelty of the persecution of Poles in the Soviet Union but also its uniqueness, which allows it to be placed on a par with the Holocaust of the Jews. The successive waves of repression of Poles by the Soviet Union are compared to the German extermination policy towards Jews. Right-wing memory discourse interprets the Soviet Union's politics as aiming at the annihilation of the Polish nation, suggesting that Poles were murdered, locked up in gulags, and sent deep into the

USSR just because they were Poles (BB, 2009). At the same time, memory politics polonises the victims of Soviet repression; for example, the 1939–1941 deportations into the USSR are presented as the martyrdom of ethnic Poles only, although there were a disproportionate number of Jews among the deportees (Jaskulowski & Majewski, 2023).

References to the situation of Jews also appear in the case of 'cursed soldiers'. For example, during the aforementioned parliamentary discussion on the commemoration of Łupaszka in 2006, a PiS MP evoked a discourse on two totalitarianisms by comparing the attitude towards Jews and cursed soldiers:

> the image of cursed soldiers constructed in this way, there is an overriding similarity to the image of the Jew created in the Third Reich (…) of a filthy, caricatured half-man who is driven by the lowest instincts, greedy, dirty, brutal, deceitful (…) after all the Nazis were only the younger brothers of the communist system.
>
> (Sejm, 2006)

The MP's statement also fits in with the thesis propounded by many right-wing politicians that Nazism has its roots in Marxist ideology (OKO Press, 2020). In accordance with this right-wing belief, Nazism is excluded from the right-wing political tradition and projected onto the left, which poses the greatest threat to humanity (Jaskulowski & Majewski, 2022).

The struggle of the 'cursed soldiers' has also been compared to the Jewish uprising in the Warsaw Ghetto. Both during public speeches and in interviews, employees of memorial institutions stressed that the cursed soldiers, like the Jews, were doomed to extermination. The communists organised 'death squads' to track them down and murder them. Like the ghetto insurgents, the 'cursed soldiers' chose a desperate struggle and an honourable death with arms in hand. In this context, 'cursed soldiers' function as a symbol of the heroic and persecuted Polish nation, constituting an allegory of its post-war fate ('cursed soldiers' as the Polish nation). The history of cursed soldiers in the dominant discourse of memory is part of Polish wartime martyrdom, which one right-wing columnist described as 'Polocaust' by proposing the construction of a proper museum (Masters & Mortensen, 2018). It should be noted here that two iconic representations of 'cursed soldiers', namely the already mentioned Pilecki and 'Inka', occupy a central place in the hegemonic memory politics – they are concrete symbols linking the two totalitarianisms and are used in the discourse of competition for suffering.

As we have already mentioned, Inka was a nurse and courier in the partisan grouping commanded by 'Łupaszka', who is responsible for crimes against the Lithuanian and Belarusian populations. Hegemonic memory politics emphasises that she was arrested by the communists and, despite being tortured, did not hand over her partisan comrades. She was sentenced to death but did not apply for clemency. She was – as is strongly emphasised – only 17 years old at the time. Memory politics constructs Inka in the convention of a secular saint – a young, innocent, and good girl (she provided help even to enemies by bandaging wounded communists). It seems that the fact that it was Inka who became so popular is not a coincidence but is due to the fact that the nurse fits perfectly into the discourse of emphasising the innocence and suffering of the Polish nation. According to the logic of the symbolism of 'cursed soldiers', Inka's words 'I behaved as I should' also draw the line between heroes and opportunists and traitors, representing determination and readiness to die for the nation (Am, 2023). The symbol of Inka – whose construction shows similarities to Sophie Scholl (activist of German anti-Nazi resistance movement White Rose sentenced to death) – illustrates the cruelty of the communists who, like the Nazis, condemned even young girls to death. Inka is an allegory of the fate of the innocent persecuted Polish nation. As one of our interviewees bluntly and briefly put it, 'communists tortured and tormented Inka because they hated what she fought for, they wanted to kill Poland'.

The figure of Pilecki, who was in the AK during the Second World War and after the war was active in the anti-communist underground, creating underground structures, is also very characteristic. Pilecki did not take part in fighting after the war, and his activities consisted of establishing an intelligence network. He considered armed resistance pointless (Bojko, 2020, p. 17). Pilecki was arrested by the communists and sentenced to death in a show trial. Although Pilecki did not belong to a partisan unit, memory politics presents him as a 'cursed soldier' (Bojko, 2020, p. 17). At the same time, the hegemonic discourse constructs Pilecki as a 'volunteer to Auschwitz' who voluntarily allowed himself to be imprisoned in the camp in order to report on the situation there and organise the underground (however, some historians dispute that this was his decision; Cuber-Strutyńska, 2014). Memory politics emphasises that he was the first to inform the West about the Holocaust, pushing aside Jan Karski, who also gave such reports. Karski, however, lived to see the Third Republic and had good relations with the post-communist left, so for the right he is not a convenient figure. Pilecki as a memorial symbol also represents the struggle against two totalitarianisms and even suggests that communism was worse than Nazism. Memory politics often quotes Pilecki's words from the period of the UB investigation, 'Auschwitz was a trifle', intended to illustrate the greater cruelty of the communists. The symbol of Pilecki is also significant in the context of Polish-Jewish relations, representing the attitude of Poles towards Jews (as we have seen, an institution documenting how Poles helped Jews was named after Pilecki). In this context, Pilecki denotes the heroism of Poles helping Jews (he risked his life to inform the world about the Holocaust) and absolves Poles of responsibility for crimes against Jews by implicitly pointing to the sins of the West – the Poles, after all, informed the West, which knew about, and did nothing to prevent, the Holocaust (Jaskulowski & Majewski, 2023).

Paradoxically, Pilecki has become a hero of football ultras who make no secret of their anti-Semitism. We should mention here the tifos display prepared by the supporters of Śląsk Wrocław in 2012, which was later reproduced on various right-wing websites. The banner bore an image of Pilecki signed 'a volunteer to Auschwitz' and with the distorted quote 'Auschwitz was a trifle compared to them'. The pronoun 'them' referred to the names on the second banner entitled 'We know the murderers of the Polish Nation', which listed the 'proper' names of security services employees, suggesting their Jewish origins, including the name of the half-brother of Adam Michnik, chief editor of *Gazeta Wyborcza*, which the extreme right calls 'Jewish', while the mainstream right uses the euphemistic term 'Polish-speaking' (Fronda, 2012). What the official memory politics only implies or expresses allusively the football supporters expressed explicitly: they contrasted the Polish nation symbolised by Pilecki with the Jews represented by the communists, evoking the stereotype of Judeo-Communism. The juxtaposition of Pilecki with the Jews highlights the ingratitude and perfidy of the Jews, who murdered a man who risked his own life to save them. The football supporters' tifo display can be dismissed as an extreme example of an unrepresentative milieu, but similar statements appear on right-wing websites and in mainstream politics, and the myth of the Jewish Commune is invoked by IPN historians (Bodakowski, 2019; Do Rzeczy, 2018). For example, the IPN vice-president gave an interview to an anti-Semitic activist, former Catholic priest Jack Międlar, who appeals to Nazi rhetoric. The vice-president suggested that Judeo-Communism was a fact (Flieger, 2019). Also, in the course of our research, some interviewees with clearly right-wing views spoke of the 'Jewisation' of the UB or even that 'the Jews killed Pilecki'.

In the context of competition for suffering, it is necessary to mention the research of psychologists who identified the existence of anti-Semitic attitudes in Poland, which they termed 'secondary anti-Semitism'. This secondary anti-Semitism is a form of anti-Jewish prejudice consisting in competing in suffering and denying that there were Poles who murdered Jews (Bilewicz et al., 2018, p. 7). It constitutes a socially acceptable form of Holocaust denial and a camouflaged way of expressing anti-Semitic attitudes (Bilewicz et al., 2018, p. 16). Psychologists argue that this secondary anti-Semitism exists as a kind of latent cognitive structure that is activated in certain situations (Bilewicz et al., 2018, pp. 8, 38). At the level of discourse, however, the difference between covert and overt anti-Semitism is not always evident, as we have seen. The belittling of Jewish suffering is at the same time accompanied, as we have seen, by anti-Semitic statements accusing Jews of the introduction of communism in Poland, for example, which can be interpreted as a form of conspiracy thinking. What distinguishes this secondary anti-Semitism is rather that, even if it refers to anti-Jewish stereotypes, it does not use overtly biological language, which is reminiscent of the phenomenon of covert or symbolic racism in Western Europe and the USA (Jaskulowski & Majewski, 2023).

Psychologists have little to say about the status of this hidden anti-Semitism. Where does it hide when it is 'dormant'? What happens to it when it is not activated (Billig, 1995)? This secondary anti-Semitism needs to be seen in the broader context of historical anti-Semitism and the dominant structures of Polish national identity, which are based on various forms of racism, often overlooked in analyses of Polish nationalisms (Balogun, 2018, 2022; Jaskulowski, 2021). Conventional wisdom states that Poland is a country free from racism, which is projected onto Western Europe and North America (Balogun, 2018; Nowicka & Łodziński, 2001). A myth rooted in romantic origins still dominates public consciousness, suggesting that since Poles themselves were victims of the imperialist powers in the 19th century, they could not have been colonisers themselves. Nevertheless, the elites participated in the circulation of European thought and were not immune to dominant Orientalist colonial patterns, drawing on racial ideas from the 'imperial cloud' (Grzechnik, 2020). Recent research shows that 19th-century imperial racism, Orientalism, scientific racism, eugenic ideas, and biological anti-Semitism were not marginal phenomena but closely related to nation-building processes in Central-Eastern Europe, including the territories of Poland, and later in the newly formed Polish nation-state after 1918 (Balogun, 2022). The growing tendency at the beginning of the 20th century to biologise social sciences and nationalist ideologies, the biologisation of anti-Semitism, coincided with the formation of nations in the region. This translated into an emphasis on the racial basis of the forming nations, which found expression in relation to the Jews, whom the nationalist right considered to be racially alien representatives of Eastern civilisation, who could not be assimilated and who threatened a healthy national body (Böhler, 2018; Gauden, 2019; Krzywiec, 2016; Turda & Weindling, 2007).

Poland has a legacy of participation in Orientalist colonial imaginaries, which is not an aberration or epiphenomenon but is ingrained in the dominant structures of Polish national identity, as confirmed by a number of recent studies. Earlier research suggested that Polish national identity was relatively open and based mainly on cultural and political factors. However, under the influence of our critique, sociologists have started examining the biological foundations of Polish identity (Jaskulowski, 2021). Recent studies based on a representative sample have shown that 54.8% of Poles believe that having white skin is a requirement for being recognised as Polish (Grodecki, 2021). The role of racialisation in defining Polishness is also indicated by research on the experiences of people of colour living in Poland and on Poles' attitudes towards migrants who are excluded from the Polish nation based on skin colour (Balogun, 2022). The significance of racial hierarchies is also evident in studies on right-wing politics and the 'migration crisis' in Poland (Jaskulowski, 2019). Some studies have argued that anti-Islamism taps into older racial patterns of anti-Semitism (Bobako, 2017; Narkowicz, 2018; Narkowicz & Pędziwiatr 2017). However, another interpretation is possible: both anti-Semitism and anti-Islamism are manifestations of the same racist logic inherent in the dominant ideology of Polish national identity, which was shaped in terms of opposition between the Polish nation (representing European civilisation) and the Orientalised Eastern civilisation defined in racial terms.

In this context, nationalist memory politics, centred around 'cursed soldiers', gains an additional dimension. As we have argued, the symbol of 'cursed soldiers' fulfils two basic, interrelated functions. On the one hand, it constitutes an allegory of the fate of the Polish nation (the Polish nation as 'cursed soldiers'). This symbol depicts the resistance of the Polish nation and its suffering. On the other hand, the symbol of 'cursed soldiers' represents the national boundaries separating 'us' and 'them' ('cursed soldiers' as the Polish nation), which are constructed around several processes of symbolic thickening. In the light of our analysis, there is another process of signification behind this symbol that is not apparent at first glance, namely racialisation. The symbol of the 'cursed soldiers' marks the boundaries between 'us' and communism, which is externalised and attributed to other peoples, especially the Jews (but also other, especially 'Eastern', nationalities), whom Polish nationalism has traditionally orientalised as non-European others, belonging to some barbaric, Eastern and inferior civilisation. In this context, 'cursed soldiers' as a key symbol of national collective memory implicitly marks the boundary that separated us from the barbaric East.

Rap Music

Attention must also be paid to popular culture, which PiS uses to promote its concept of collective memory. Popular culture plays an important role in the reproduction of national identity due to its ubiquity (Edensor, 2002). We interpret popular culture as a space of meanings, symbols, and emotions that is the object of an ideological 'positional war' for cultural hegemony (Gramsci, 1999). Pop culture can provide political ideologies with a set of meanings, images, and narratives that are impactful through the power of their universality and obviousness. Contemporary political actors are keen to use popular culture to promote their vision of the national community (Edensor, 2002). This strategy can be described as cultural incorporation, involving the control of pop-cultural imaginaries so as to modify them according to a hegemonic project and use them to stabilise hegemonic power, while marginalising oppositional meanings (Fiske, 2011).

An example of such incorporation is PiS politics towards so-called 'patriotic rap', which has become one of the main pop-cultural vehicles of narratives and emotions centred around the symbolism of the 'cursed soldiers'. Paradoxically, music originally associated with African-American resistance culture became a means of expression of Polish nationalism (Neal, 1999). Rap in the process of glocalisation was adapted in other cultural contexts, including Poland in the 1990s. Early Polish rappers focused on social exclusion, poverty, unemployment, street life, and conflict with the law. Their songs evoked an aura of contestation against dominant values and social norms. Mainstream media portrayed rap as a kind of anti-music, a manifestation of plebeian aesthetic tastes, and identified it with the subculture of the yobbo, residents of socialist tower blocks who refused to adapt to the capitalist reality (Majewski, 2018; Miszczyński, 2014; Mitchell, 2001). Since the beginning of the 21st century, rap has gone mainstream and has gradually become one of the most popular music genres among young people. A survey conducted in 2018 found that rap was listened to by 59% of young people aged 12 to 17, making it the second-favourite genre for young people after pop, which was listened to by 62% of respondents (Kukułowicz, 2019).

With its growing popularity, rap began to undergo a process of incorporation. Rap became an object of interest not only for mainstream media wishing to sell their products to 'young' people but also for various political actors seeking to capitalise on its growing popularity (Majewski, 2018, 2021). As a result, some rappers, seeing an opportunity to advance their careers, moved from street themes to national-historical topics and established cooperation with various memory politics institutions such as the IPN or the Museum of the AK in Cracow. One of the more popular rappers who have undertaken such collaboration is 'Tadek' (Tadeusz Polkowski), who was initially a gangsta rapper (he had his own clothing brand, JP, which is a Polish abbreviation for 'Fuck the Police') and later became the main representatives of 'patriotic rap' (Majewski, 2018). It would seem that his street production is at odds with his role as a guardian of national memory. Yet, its transformation can be seen as an example of the process of incorporation of subjugated group culture by dominant institutions. The right-wing media began to portray rap as an example of genuine countercultural opposition to the socially unjust and anti-national III RP. From this perspective, gangster themes are grassroots expressions of rebellion against a decadent culture and lack of perspectives, which only needs to be properly channelled.

Although PiS politicians do not refer to the work of rappers directly, the cultural institutions they control support them in many ways. PiS promotes patriotic hip-hop indirectly, as rap is still generally regarded as an example of low culture and a manifestation of plebeian taste. On the one hand, this shows the power of the popular aesthetic, but, on the other hand, it indicates that pop culture is still treated with a certain distrust and distance (Majewski, 2021). The fact that PiS does not openly refer to rap is beneficial for both the rappers and the party itself. Nationalist rappers can continue to create their songs in a convention of anti-establishment contestation, while contributing to the construction of PiS hegemony. Unlike the early rappers, patriotic rappers make little mention of economic and social issues, focusing mainly on historical themes. They sing and speak in mainstream media about national decline, the destruction of Polish identity by internal enemies and European 'leftist' and cosmopolitan elites, and the need for a national revolution. For example, in response to the 'migration crisis', they began to rap about the alleged Muslim threat to the Polish nation, threatening the 'invaders' with ethnic cleansing (Jaskulowski, 2019; Majewski, 2017). Thus, the message of rap is often more blunt and explicit, even if this is partially coincidental, than the hegemonic ideology. By promoting 'patriotic' rap, PiS strengthens its hegemonic ideological position, but at the same time it opens a space for the radicalisation of right-wing nationalism, e.g. by normalising the rhetoric of violence.

An important element of the rappers' production is historical themes related to 'cursed soldiers'. 'Cursed soldiers' function in this nationalist pop culture as 'national forms of representation' that enable individuals to identify with an 'imagined community' (Edensor, 2002). They serve to represent the ethnocultural boundaries of the nation, while also acting as exemplary instances of 'true' Polishness. One can distinguish five functions that rap performs in the hegemonic project of memory politics. First, in line with the logic of the PiS memory politics, 'patriotic' rap plays a differentiating function, which consists in reinforcing the perception of the world in dichotomous categories of 'us' (true Poles) and 'them' (strangers and traitors). Second, it performs an emotional function by conveying emotions such as a sense of threat, anxiety, fear, resentment, pride, respect, or recognition. Third, it has the function of motivating people to take action in the name of the nation. Fourth, it has an integrating function by constructing group and individual identity around the symbol of the 'cursed soldiers'. Fifth, it fulfils a compensatory function by constituting a specific discursive response to the deep longing for a 'real' fight against the 'real' enemy, which would allow rappers to realise the model of male heroism imposed by the dominant culture.

The differentiating function takes the form of an essentialising discourse that constructs binary oppositions, which it naturalises and de-historicises. The discourse attributes unambiguously positive qualities to one component of the opposition and negative qualities to the other. In the 'patriotic' rap, everything symbolised by the 'cursed soldiers' represents only positive qualities, while everything opposed to them has negative (and simultaneously non-Polish) qualities. Rap equates different historical events and presents contemporary events as a repetition of earlier ones, as the same struggle of Poles against the enemies of Polishness. It allows rappers to use the symbol of 'cursed soldiers' for the current struggle for cultural hegemony. The rappers present the 'cursed soldiers' as a model of Polishness, and themselves as their heirs. In their lyrics, Poland after 1989 is the folwark of post-communist elites – who are the heirs of those who murdered the 'cursed soldiers'.

For example, a song 'Lemming' by artists Ciech, Pjus, Kamel, conveys a narrative contrasting post-1989 Poland with its historical past. The artists critique the post-communist elite, whom they perceive as manipulators of both power and public perception, akin to their predecessors who opposed the 'cursed soldiers'. The song draws parallels between current societal struggles and historical conflicts, emphasising a continuous fight for cultural power in Poland. The 'cursed soldiers' are depicted as symbols of true Polish values and resistance against oppression, and the rappers position themselves as modern-day successors to these figures. The song suggests that contemporary Polish society is still influenced by communist-era ideologies and that the media plays a significant role in shaping public opinion and historical narratives. The overall theme revolves around the enduring impact of historical events on present-day Poland and the ongoing struggle to uphold right-wing ideals of Polishness against perceived threats.

The emotional function is primarily to arouse fear of the denationalisation and extermination of Poles. The rappers eagerly evoke the notion of the 'Polocaust', of which Poland was supposed to have fallen victim many times in the past. The last phase of the Polocaust has been going on since 1989 and consists of an attempt to culturally annihilate Poles. According to the rappers, no overthrow of communism has taken place – only the form of communist domination has changed. The coalition of post-communists, liberals, leftists and Brussels elites seeks to erase the national memory among Poles and to undermine national solidarity. However, attempts to annihilate Poles have failed, because the self-sacrifice of the 'cursed soldiers' has become the seed of moral renewal – a source of inspiration for today's patriots. Thus, the song 'Cursed Soldiers' by Tadek highlights the fear of cultural and physical annihilation of the Polish people, a concept referred to as the holocaust by the artist. This term is used to describe various historical periods where Poland faced existential threats. The song suggests that since the fall of communism in 1989, Poland has been undergoing process of cultural eradication orchestrated by a coalition of post-communists, liberals, leftists, and certain European elites. The song emphasises that despite these challenges, the spirit of the 'cursed soldiers' continues to inspire modern patriots. The 'cursed soldiers' are depicted as a symbol of moral resilience and a source of spiritual renewal. The artist conveys a message of enduring struggle and resistance, suggesting that the legacy of these historical figures is re-emerging in contemporary times to counteract the perceived threats to Polish identity and sovereignty.

'Patriotic' rap has a mobilising function because its task is to motivate the recipients to take action to regain control over the life of the national community. The rappers present themselves as the heirs of the 'cursed soldiers', who face similar repression. This is why the figure of the 'patriot football fan' who sits in prison often appears in their work. Fans serve sentences for involvement in violent crimes, drug trafficking, etc., but rappers frame this as persecution for patriotic activity. Paradoxically, although PiS preaches the ideal of tough law and order, right-wing politicians have many times defended stadium hooligans in an attempt to win over the sympathies of this community. According to the rappers, football fans are fighting the system and are one of the few to oppose the cultural 'Polocaust', while the liberal media turn them into 'thugs' and 'neo-Nazis'. What we have here is a kind of postcolonial discourse: the rappers see themselves as the continuators of the 'eternal struggle' against the internal and external colonisers of the Polish nation. They construct themselves as successive members of the national relay of heroes.

The integrating function of rap lies in the discursive construction of group and individual identity. This imagery is meant to unite people who share the rappers' vision of the world, and songs dedicated to the 'cursed soldiers' set the order of things, i.e. direct attention to selected events, give them specific meanings and marginalise others. The integrative function of these identity narratives is thus to reproduce in pop-cultural form perceptions, values and views in line with the right-wing memory politics. The aim is to reunite Poles with lasting national bonds and to revive their national 'spirit'. In this sense, the pop-cultural memory politics reproduced by rappers is an element of the mythical-symbolic complex, which is a set of national forms of representation intended to consolidate and integrate Poles. An important role of the integrating function of this pop-cultural discourse is the reproduction of the nationalist ideal of the Polish male hero-patriot in accordance with the logic of the ideology of hegemonic masculinity. Traditionally, nationalisms have had a distinctly gendered dimension manifested especially in the production of unequal power relations that perpetuate male dominance (Enloe, 1998; Mosse, 1988; Nagel, 1998; Yuval-Davis, 1997). It emphasised the fundamental role of 'masculine' qualities underpinning the existence and survival of the national community (Nagel, 1998). From its beginnings, Polish nationalism also accorded a privileged social position to men. It constructed a mythical image of national organisations composed of brave and honourable men united by bonds of brotherhood, who sacrificed their lives fighting for the freedom of the fatherland (paradoxically often imagined transgressively as a woman, a mother – a passive object of male concern) (Grzebalska, 2013).

In 'patriotic rap', the symbol of the 'cursed soldiers' is a metaphor for male brotherhood, which serves to reproduce the traditional model of Polish masculinity, based on the idea of a community of heroic warriors protecting 'their' women. This symbolism of the male brotherhood also reproduces the motif of a male subculture community that is archetypal for hip-hop culture. 'Cursed soldiers' are portrayed as archetypal 'bros', loyal to their group and ready to fight against the system. 'Patriot rappers', in their view, reproduce the masculine 'ethos' of the 'cursed soldiers' community. They evoke stories about male heroes, which are like 'lives of saints', summaries of their lives, the 'miracles' they performed and other heroic deeds. It is worth noting their monotony and repetitiveness due to the fact that they are hagiographic reworkings of Wikipedia biographies. They can be summarised in a few points: they fought for Poland's freedom and values close to every 'real Pole', their enemies were communists (soviets, traitors, and Jews), they fought to the end; they died fighting or were sentenced to torture and death, they lost, but thanks to the rappers, the memory of them has survived and inspires people to act today, giving hope of a national rebirth.

The male community symbolised by the 'cursed soldiers', on the one hand, represents the dominant position of men in nationalist discourse, constructing an image of a male-dominant community, and, on the other hand, it performs important compensatory functions. Nationalist rap can be interpreted as an expression of a specific form of melancholy and 'displaced desire'. It expresses a longing for war and struggle that the rappers never personally experienced. As Klaus Theweleit has written, for men marked by this type of melancholy, fighting for the nation is a condition of the obtaining of a masculine 'soul' (Theweleit, 1987). Thus, a war is the most important measure of masculinity and masculine value. One can risk the thesis that 'patriotic rappers' evoking images of bloody war, torture, and executions are in a sense compensating for their lack of actual combat experience and their 'incomplete masculinity'. From this perspective, one can also look at the links between patriotic rap and football hooligans, who find in rap's historical rhetoric an ennoblement of stadium violence. Hooligan violence may be seen as compensation for the lack of war experience and as part of the process of becoming a real man. German male youth joining the Nazi movement in the 1930s were characterised by a similar sense of melancholy. Young Germans had not been able to participate in the First World War and thus, many of them felt, had missed the opportunity to prove that they were fully fledged men. They took an obsessive interest in war literature cultivating an idealised image of male life in the trenches, which became the object of their longing. In this way, the experience of war was transformed into nostalgia for male friendship (Mosse, 1988).

This rappers' longing for the life of a male war hero is merely a radicalisation of a wider tendency. The dominant historical narrative in Poland is centred on the armed deeds of male heroes who sacrifice themselves in the name of the nation. This narrative is reproduced in various forms at all levels of formal education, perpetuated in the 'great' canonical cultural works and reproduced in popular culture. It is dominated by a male pattern of wartime heroism, which, however, is not easily realised today (Jaskulowski et al., 2022). Rap focused on 'cursed soldiers' can be read as an expression of longing for a 'real' fight against a 'real' enemy, which would allow them to fulfil the dominant model of heroism and masculinity. Thanks to the discursive confrontation with everything that threatens 'Polishness', these men, deprived of the possibility of real fighting, can stand in the row of great heroes and play the role of 'real' men who sacrifice themselves in the name of their nation.

In this context, it is necessary to mention the role of women, to whom traditionally Polish nationalism assigned secondary roles and enclosed femininity in the figure of the 'sanctified' mother (Grzebalska, 2013). The origins of this process can be traced back to the proto-national period and the nobility's metaphors of familial kinship between 'lords-brothers' and idealised images of femininity in the form of the figure of the Virgin who was proclaimed Queen of Poland in the 17th century. Later, these images became nationalised and biologised, taking the form of naturalistic representations of the fatherland

and the nation as a community united by blood ties (Ostrowska, 2004). Nationalist rappers often align themselves with a patriarchal-nationalist view of gender roles and frequently allude to concepts of a national community bonded by blood and the imagery of a nation as a mother. For instance, Basti in his song 'We are Poles' highlights the brotherhood and blood ties that unite Polish men and underscores their duty to protect their metaphorical mother, Poland. He claims his place in a lineage of male Polish national heroes who have historically defended their 'mother' nation. Additionally, the rappers utilise the mother metaphor to draw a distinction: 'us' and those they perceive as lacking in patriotism. Evtis, in his track 'Today I go to fight, Mum', illustrates this by portraying Poland as a mother figure revered by her sons, who are committed to defending her, contrasting those who respect her with traitors who do not. This metaphor extends to a personal commitment to fight for the nation, likened to supporting and protecting one's own mother.

Rap lyrics portray Poland as being in a deep crisis: the mother nation is threatened by various internal and external enemies. In this context, it is necessary to note, following Maria Janion (2006), that in Polish nationalist discourse the attitude to the mother nation is characterised by ambivalence, which reveals itself in moments of danger. This ambivalence consists in the fact that in the nationalist imagination, the relationship between the motherland and the son is replaced by lovers relationship. This 'tanatic-incestuous-perverse transgression' can be seen in the work of Tadek Polkowski. In his works, he portrays girls involved in the PPP who are described as being physically appealing and attractive. Their resolve and steadfastness evoke a sense of admiration and a desire for both emotional and erotic intimacy among their patriotic male counterparts. Tadek conveys this through imagery of a woman whose eyes are fearless, bright, and fiery, invoking a sense of warmth and safety in their presence. He speaks of intimate scenarios, like walking together in the forest and sitting by a fire while the woman sings a song. These scenes serve to illustrate a deeper emotional connection and support among these characters, as exemplified by a man seeking courage in the gaze of Inka when feeling fearful about fighting.

The heroine's corporeality plays a major role in this story: her raped, beaten, tortured body represents the humiliated nation. The image of a tortured nation stimulated patriots to fight the enemy, but also aroused a sadomasochistic erotic fascination (Janion, 2006). In his song 'The little AK girl', Polkowski paints a picture of a heroine who, despite being elevated to an angelic status, possesses earthly, sensual characteristics that stir a longing for physical closeness in men. The protagonist expresses a wish to embrace her to provide warmth, highlighting her vulnerability. She is depicted as a young member of the AK, adorned with symbols of valour and femininity, and she appears in his dreams with a captivating smile. This young woman, along with others like her, is portrayed as being so pure and ethereal in their heroism that they transcend humanity, becoming angelic beings amidst the harsh realities of war. Yet, despite their perceived divinity, they face brutal realities, being targeted, and martyred by Nazis and communists. The protagonist's desire to comfort and protect these figures is repeatedly expressed, showing a yearning to reconnect with and safeguard these immaculate yet afflicted young women from their tragic fates.

Polkowski's songs are a manifestation of a discourse of concern that reveals another aspect of how 'patriotic rappers' perceive femininity, in line with the logic of masculinist nationalism. Polkowski assigns strictly defined roles to women in his songs. In Tadek's portrayal, the young female AK partisans are characterised less by their heroic actions and more by qualities such as angelic purity, innocence, and youthful femininity. These attributes make them passive and delicate, consequently portraying them as reliant on male protection. In his narrative, the protagonist encounters a young girl named Inka in his dreams and he feels a strong urge to protect her, emphasising her youth and vulnerability. This dreamlike interaction underscores a protective stance towards these young women, culminating in a call to aggressors to refrain from harming these innocent figures. This representation reflects a broader theme where the valour of these young women is overshadowed by their perceived fragility and need for male guardianship. The active actors in this story are men, especially the rapper himself who defend and hug the little AK angels. It is the men who fight for freedom, their honour, their homeland, and 'their' women (Nagel, 1998). The antagonists, however, are other men, who take away 'their little girls' from 'us'. Polkowski's work reproduces the image of the 'natural' domination of men belonging to the public and active world of 'culture' over submissive women, whose domain is supposed to be the space of 'nature' and the family. At the same time, in this story the myth of the male warrior, whose mentality is shaped on the categorical separation of the masculine from the feminine, is manifested (Theweleit, 1987). 'The little AK girls', in fact, represent all those qualities that the 'warrior-patriot' must eliminate from his own life if he wants to preserve his masculinity.

One can distinguish three ways in which rap songs about 'cursed soldiers' construct women's place in the national community. These are interrelated topoi that, in line with Polish hegemonic culture, reduce women to an object of male domination (Enloe, 1998). The first topos is the representation of women in objectifying terms as a valuable property of the nation, which is vulnerable to exploitation by others from whom this national asset must be defended. Women are passive and defenceless bodies described in terms of objects that are possessed, conquered, and regained by men. The function of women here, then, is merely to use them as symbols of rival male systems of rule (Theweleit, 1987). In the second topos, women function as kinds of ethnic transmitters, and their role is reduced to giving birth. They are most often represented through the figures of the mothers or wives of the 'cursed soldiers'. Although seemingly not mentioned here, female sexuality is the main focus as a matter of national honour. The symbolic boundaries of the nation are constructed in terms of women's appropriate sexual behaviour, and national honour in terms of men's ability to control women's behaviour (Enloe, 1998). Finally, in the third of these topoi, women are presented as instruments for transmitting national culture and for raising new generations of patriots. Here they become mainly the transmitters of national identity.

Patriotic rappers present themselves as anti-systemic artists contesting the existing political order, which might suggest that they constitute something like the kind of 'counter-hegemonic' memory leaders that Foucault (1977) wrote about. In reality, however, they are to a large extent 'sellers' of the hegemonic memory politics. They adapt the hegemonic memory politics to the pop-cultural aesthetic by selling it in the guise of anti-establishment rebellion. Their work can therefore be seen in terms of incorporation rather than some kind of bottom-up resistance by subordinated groups. Nationalist rap does not serve to pluralise Polish collective memory or express some kind of counter-memory of subordinated groups. 'Patriotic rappers' do not convey any alternative order of knowledge that is marginalised by the dominant discourse. Their work relies on the use of hegemonic narratives about the past, which they recycle according to a pop-cultural aesthetic (Adamski, 2012).

An important element used in the process of incorporation of rap is also the promotion of a specific style of clothing through it, referred to as 'patriotic clothing'. For the companies selling it, 'patriotic rap' has become an important aspect of marketing strategy. These companies sponsor rappers who advertise their products on their records, in their music videos and at concerts, which collaborate with leading rappers. The most popular companies are Patriotic, Surge Polonia, or Pro Patriae, and especially Red is Bad. For example, the latter company cooperates with, among others, the IPN and the Museum of the Second World War, selling its products in museum shops and participating in various educational projects. The company made headlines when President Andrzej Duda wore a T-shirt with the company's name printed on it when flying on an official visit to China in 2015. Red is Bad's website includes a Manifesto that aligns with dominant memory politics and targets a specific customer base. The Manifesto emphasises that the brand caters to individuals who cherish freedom and take pride in Polish history. It highlights a commitment to celebrating heroes who are often overlooked, focusing on the Polish resistance against Soviet rule. The brand takes pride in the fact that Poland had resilient fighters who continued their underground armed struggle against communists until 1963. Emphasising national pride, the Manifesto concludes with a statement about the brand's dedication to Polish production and quality, underscoring its alignment with national values and history (RedisBad, 2018). This nationalist spirit of capitalism represented by Red is Bad and other producers of 'patriotic clothing' is based on the sale of consumer goods intended to symbolise 'true Polishness'.

The 'patriotic' clothing and gadgets they sell (such as bedding, mugs, underwear, bags, towels, caps, patches, thermoses, etc.) are branded with national 'figures of memory' that refer to various historical military events, male heroes of the figures ranging from Mieszko to 'cursed soldiers', including those accused of crimes. The garments also bear anti-Ukrainian, anti-Lithuanian, anti-communist, anti-Muslim, and anti-European slogans. This clothing nationalism reinforces the rappers' message by defining Polishness in terms of Catholicism, a male patriarchal community of blood. It exposes the symbolism of blood and glorifies the sacrifice of life and killing in the name of the nation (one of the more popular slogans is 'Death to the enemies of the fatherland'). It manifests a sense of pride in the military achievements of male ancestors. There is a very clear tendency to define Polishness in opposition to some 'other', as well as historical revanchism and nostalgia for the Polish 'eastern borderlands'. In this way, clothing becomes an aesthetic object of high axiological concentration and begins to play the role of nationalistic fetishes (Jaskulowski & Majewski, 2016). The possession of these fetishes enables their consumers to access a conscious experiencing of national identity. As rapper Evtis explains, 'someone will like a hoodie, buy it, wear it, and in a while they will become interested in the theme itself (…) attend some meeting with historians, buy some book' (Ada, 2017). In this way, manifesting one's national identity also becomes possible through attachment to specific clothing brands or presenting oneself with various 'patriotic' gadgets. This pop-nationalist consumerism, straight from the shopping mall, becomes not so much a 'lifestyle' as a 'style of dress', which reflects the process of commodification of national identity. Manufacturers of 'patriotic clothing' are well aware of this, arguing as part of their advertising strategies that the purchase and wearing of the products they offer is a kind of patriotic activity to bring nationalist ideas to life. As one shop's website proclaims, 'remember every single penny you spend in the ProPatriae shop is a brick on the foundation of Great Poland!' (http://propatriae.pl/strona/o-nas).

References

Ada. (2017). Wywiad z Evtisem [Interview with Etvis]. *Kierunki*. Retrieved from https://kierunki.info.pl/wywiad-z-evtisem/

Adamski, Ł. (2012). Tadek, niewygodna prawda, tak powinno się uczyć patriotyzmu [Tadek, inconvenient truth, this is how patriotism should be taught]. *Wpolityce*. Retrieved from https://wpolityce.pl/kultura/246777-tadek-niewygodna-prawda-tak-powinno-uczyc-sie-patriotyzmu-recenzja

Aleszumm. (2014). Stop praniu mózgów, zatajane wstydliwe fakty o Komorowskim, dziadek Komorowskiego rezun [Stop the brainwashing, the concealed shameful facts about Komorowski, Komorowski's grandfather rezun]. Retrieved from https://niepoprawni.pl/blog/2218/stop-praniu-mozgow-zatajane-wstydliwe-fakty-o-komorowskim-dziadek-komorowskiego-rezun

Alexander, J. C. (2006). Cultural pragmatics: Social performance between ritual and strategy. In J. C. Alexander, B. Giesen, & J. L. Mast (Eds.), *Social performance. Symbolic action, cultural pragmatics, and ritual* (pp. 29–90). Cambridge: Cambridge University Press.

Am. (2023, March 2). W Gdańsku poświęcono bursztynowe serce w hołdzie dla Danuty Siedzikówny "Inki" [An amber heart was consecrated in Gdansk in tribute to Danuta Siedzikówna"Inka"]. *RadioGdańsk*. Retrieved from https://radiogdansk.pl/wiadomosci/region/trojmiasto/2023/03/02/w-gdansku-poswiecono-bursztynowe-serce-w-holdzie-dla-danuty-siedzikowny-inki/

Ambroziak, A. (2009, February 27). 1 marca dla żołnierzy niepodległości [1 March for independence soldiers]. *Nasz Dziennik*. Retrieved from https://stary.naszdziennik.pl/bpl_index.php?typ=po&dat=20090227&id=po61.txt

Arseniuk, A., & Musiał, F. (Eds.). (2015). *Rzeczpospolita wolnych ludzi. Janusz Kurtyka w mediach [The Republic of Free People: Janusz Kurtyka in the media]*. Warsaw: IPN.

Balogun, B. (2018). Polish lebensraum: The colonial ambition to expand on racial terms. *Ethnic and Racial Studies*, 41(14), 2561–2579.

Balogun, B. (2022). Race, blood, and nation: The manifestation of eugenics in Central and Eastern Europe. *Ethnic and Racial Studies*, 45(13), 2478–2485.

BB. (2009, September 1). Prezydent: Katyń jak Holocaust [President: Katyn as the Holocaust]. *Dziennik.pl*. Retrieved from https://wiadomosci.dziennik.pl/polityka/artykuly/94206,prezydent-katyn-jak-holocaust.html

Bilewicz, M. et al. (2018). Studium Stosunku Polaków do Żydów i Historii Holocaustu w Kontekście Debaty Wokół Ustawy o IPN [A study of the attitudes of poles towards Jews and the history of the holocaust in the context of the debate regarding the IPN Law]. *Nauka*, 2, 7–41.

Bill, S. (2022). Counter-elite populism and civil society in Poland: PiS's strategies of elite replacement. *East European Politics and Societies: And Cultures*, 36(1), 118–140.

Billig, M. (1995). *Banal nationalism*. London: Sage.

Bobako, M. (2017). *Islamofobia jako technologia władzy [Islamophobia as a technology of power]*. Cracow: Universitas.

Boguszewski, M. (2017). W Orłowie na Mazurach odsłonięto Panteon Niezłomnych Żołnierzy Wyklętych [Pantheon of indomitable soldiers unveiled in Orłowo, Masuria]. *Dzieje.pl*. Retrieved from https://dzieje.pl/aktualnosci/w-orlowie-na-mazurach-odslonieto-panteon-zolnierzy-wykletych

Bodakowski, J. (2019). Rotmistrz Witold Pilecki. Niewygodna prawda dla Żydów [Rotmistrz Witold Pilecki. An inconvenient truth for Jews]. *Fronda.pl*. Retrieved from https://www.fronda.pl/a/rotmistrz-witold-pilecki-niewygodna-prawda-dla-zydow,130883.html

Böhler, J. (2018). *Civil war in Central Europe, 1918–1921: The reconstruction of Poland*. Oxford: Oxford University Press.

Bojko, Ł. (2020). *Rozstrzelane pokolenie [The executed generation]*. Cracow: eSPe.

Bratcher, I. (2020). Ideological others and national identifications in contemporary Poland. *Nations and Nationalism*, 26, 677–691.

Brubaker, R. (2017). Between nationalism and civilizationism: The European populist moment in comparative perspective. *Ethnic and Racial Studies*, 40(8), 1191–1226.

Cenckiewicz, S., & Gontarczyk, P. (2008). *SB a Lech Wałęsa. Przyczynek do biografii [SB and Lech Walesa. A contribution to biography]*. Warsaw: IPN.

Čolović, I. (2002). *The politic of identity in Serbia: Essays in political anthropology*. New York: New York University Press.

Cuber-Strutyńska, E. (2014). Witold Pilecki. Konfrontacja z Legendą o 'Ochotniku do Auschwitz' [Witold Pilecki. Confrontation with the legend of the 'volunteer to Auschwitz']. *Zagłada Żydów. Studia I Materiały, 10,* 474–494.

Dmochowska, M. (2008, June 17). List Marii Dmochowskiej do byłego prezydenta [Letter from Maria Dmochowska to the former President]. *Rzeczpospolita.* Retrieved from https://www.rp.pl/publicystyka/art16171561-list-marii-dmochowskiej-do-bylego-prezydenta

Do Rzeczy. (2018, February 3). Prof. Pawłowicz: Holokaust Polaków trwał też po II wojnie. Czy Żydzi są winni zbrodni na Polakach? [Prof. Pawłowicz: The Holocaust of Poles continued after World War II. Are Jews guilty of crimes against Poles?]. *Do Rzeczy.*

Dobrosielski, P. (2017). *Spory o Grossa [Disputes over Gross].* Warsaw: IBL.

Durkheim, É. (1912/2008]). *Elementary forms of the religious life.* London: Dover Publications.

Dybicz, P., & Woroncow, J. (2019). *Wyklęci na Podlasiu: Bury, Łupaszka, Huzar.* Warsaw: Fundacja Oratio Recta.

Edensor, T. (2002). *National identity, popular culture and everyday life.* Oxford and New York: Berg.

Engelking, B., & Grabowski, J. (2018). *Dalej jest noc: losy Żydów w wybranych powiatach okupowanej Polski [Night without end: The fates of Jews in selected counties of occupied Poland].* Warsaw: Centrum Badań nad Zagładą Żydów.

Enloe, C. (1998). *Bananas, beaches and bases: Making feminist sense of international politics.* Berkeley: University of California Press.

Fiske, J. (2011). *Understanding popular culture.* London and New York: Routledge.

Flieger, E. (2019, October 6). Wiceprezes IPN Mówi Międlarowi: Żydokomuna to Fakt Historyczny [IPN vice-president tells Międlar: Judeo-communism is an historical fact]. *Gazeta Wyborcza.* Retrieved from https://wyborcza.pl/7,75398,25279072,wiceprezes-ipn-mowi-miedlarowi-zydokomuna-to-fakt-historyczny.html

Foucault, M. (1977). *Language, counter-memory, practice: Selected essays and interviews.* Ithaca, NY: Cornell University Press.

Friszke, A. (2008, June 21–21). Zniszczyć Wałęsę [Destroy Walesa]. *Gazeta Wyborcza.* Retrieved from https://archive.ph/CKRjv

Fronda. (2012). Kibice Śląska Wrocław: Bo Oświęcim przy nich to była igraszka [Slask Wrocław supporters: Oświęcim was a trifle compared to them]. *Fronda.pl.* Retrieved from https://www.fronda.pl/a/kibice-slaska-wroclaw-bo-oswiecim-przy-nich-to-byla-igraszka,19549.html

Gajewska, J., & Zaguła, W. (2013). *Rycerze lasu. [Knights of the Forest].* Warsaw: Wydawnictwo Unum.

Gałka, E. (2013). Scenariusz uroczystości z okazji Święta Żołnierzy Wyklętych [Scenario of a ceremony on the occasion of the Day of Cursed soldiers]. Retrieved from https://lscdn.pl/pl/publikacje/publikacje-pozostale/9936,Scenariusz-uroczystosci-z-okazji-Swieta-Zolnierzy-Wykletych.html

Gauden, G. (2019). *Lwów – kres Iluzji: Opowieść o pogromie listopadowym 1918 [Lviv – The end of illusion: A story of the November 1918 pogrom].* Cracow: Universitas.

Grabowski, J. (2013). *Hunt for the Jews: Betrayal and murder in German-occupied Poland.* Bloomington: Indiana University Press.

Grabowski, J. (2021, November 28). Pamięciowy blitz Instytutu Pileckiego Dotarł do Treblinki [Pilecki Institute's commemorative blitz has reached Treblinka]. *Gazeta Wyborcza.* Retrieved from https://wyborcza.pl/alehistoria/7,162654,27852129,pamieciowy-blitz-instytutu-pileckiego-dotarl-do-treblinki.html

Gramsci, A. (1999). *Selection from the prison notebooks.* London: Electric Book Company.

Grodecki, M. (2021). Odmiany polskiej tożsamości narodowej i Ich konsekwencje dla postaw wobec mniejszości [Varieties of Polish national identity and their consequences for attitudes towards minorities]. *Studia Socjologiczne, 4*(253), 33–58.

Gross, J. T. (2001). *Neighbors: The destruction of the Jewish Community in Jedwabne, Poland.* Princeton, NJ: Princeton University Press.

Gross, J. T. (2006). *Fear: Anti-semitism in Poland after Auschwitz.* New York: Random House.

Grzebalska, W. (2013). *Płeć powstania warszawskiego [Gender of the Warsaw uprising].* Warsaw: IBL, NCK.

Grzechnik, M. (2020). Ad Maiorem Poloniae Gloriam! Polish inter-colonial encounters in Africa in the interwar period. *Journal of Imperial and Commonwealth History, 48*, 826–845.

Hackmann, J. (2018). Defending the "good name" of the Polish nation: Politics of history as a battlefield in Poland, 2015–18. *Journal of Genocide Research, 20*(4), 587–606

Hristova, M., & Żychlińska, M. (2020). Mass grave exhumations as patriotic retreat. *Human Remains and Violence, 6*(2), 42–60.

IK. (2014, February 16). NSZ o żołnierzach wyklętych [NSZ about cursed soldiers]. *Nasz Dziennik.* Retrieved from https://naszdziennik.pl/polska-kraj/68409,nsz-o-zolnierzach-wykletych.html

IPN. (2006). Twarze wrocławskiej bezpieki [Faces of the Wrocław Security services]. Retrieved from https://ipn.gov.pl/pl/edukacja-1/wystawy/13487,Twarze-wroclawskiej-bezpieki.html

IPN. (2019). Komunikat dotyczący informacji zawartych w ustaleniach końcowych śledztwa S 28/02/Zi w sprawie pozbawienia życia 79 osób – mieszkańców powiatu Bielsk Podlaski, w tym 30 osób tzw. furmanów w lesie koło Puchał Starych, dokonanych w okresie od dnia 29 stycznia 1946 r. do dnia 2 lutego 1946 r. [Communication concerning the information contained in the final findings of investigation S 28/02/Zi into the deprivation of life of 79 persons – inhabitants of Bielsk Podlaski district, including 30 so-called "carters" in the forest near Puchały Stare, carried out in the period from 29 January 1946 to 2 February 1946]. Retrieved from https://ipn.gov.pl/pl/dla-mediow/komunikaty/67471,Komunikat-dotyczacy-informacji-zawartych-w-ustaleniach-koncowych-sledztwa-S-2802.html

IPN. (2021). Scenariusz lekcji "Żołnierze Wyklęci, Żołnierze Niezłomni czy polscy bandyci?" [Lesson scenario "Cursed soldiers, Indomitable soldiers or Polish bandits?"]. Retrieved from https://Warsaw.ipn.gov.pl/waw/aktualnosci/138832,Scenariusz-lekcji-Zolnierze-Wykleci-Zolnierze-Niezlomni-czy-polscy-bandyci.html

Janion, M. (2006). *Niesamowita słowiańszczyzna [Uncanny slavdom].* Cracow: Wydawnictwo Literackie.

Jaskulowski, K. (2012). *Wspólnota symboliczna [Symbolic community].* Gdańsk: WN Katedra.

Jaskulowski, K. (2019). *The everyday politics of migration crisis in Poland.* Cham: Palgrave.

Jaskulowski, K. (2021). The politics of national identity survey: Polishness, whiteness, and racial exclusion. *Nationalities Papers, 49*(6), 1082–1092.
Jaskulowski, K., & Kilias, J. (2016). Polityka nacjonalistycznej rewolucji [The politics of nationalist revolution]. *Studio Opinii*. Retrieved from http://studioopinii.pl/archiwa/164532
Jaskulowski, K., & Majewski, P. (2016). The UEFA European Football Championship 2012 and pop nationalism in Poland: Between confirmation and contestation. *Identities, 23*(5), 555–571.
Jaskulowski, K., & Majewski, P. (2020). Politics of memory in Upper Silesian schools: Between Polish homogeneous nationalism and its Silesian discontents. *Memory Studies, 13*(1), 60–73.
Jaskulowski, K., & Majewski, P. (2022). Populist in form, nationalist in content? Law and Justice, nationalism and memory politics. *European Politics and Society*. Advanced online publication. DOI: 10.1080/23745118.2022.2058752
Jaskulowski, K., & Majewski, P. (2023). The memory politics of Cursed Soldiers, antisemitism and racialisation. *Nations and Nationalism*. Advanced online publication. DOI: https://doi.org/10.1111/nana.12937
Jaskulowski, K., Majewski, P., & Surmiak, A. (2018). Teaching the nation: History and nationalism in Polish school history education. *British Journal of Sociology of Education, 39*(1), 77–91.
Jaskulowski, K., Majewski, P., & Surmiak, A. (2022). *Teaching history, celebrating nationalism: School history education in Poland*. London and New York: Routledge.
Jaskulowski, K., & Surmiak, A. (2017). Teaching history, teaching nationalism: A qualitative study of history teachers in a Polish post-industrial town. *Critical Studies in Education, 58*(1), 36–51.
Kaczyński, L. (2009). List Prezydenta z okazji 63 rocznicy mordu żołnierzy NSZ [Letter from the President on the 63rd anniversary of the murder of NSZ soldiers]. Retrieved from https://www.prezydent.pl/kancelaria/archiwum/archiwum-lecha-kaczynskiego/aktualnosci/rok-2009/list-prezydenta-z-okazji-63-rocznicy-mordu-zolnierzy-nsz,25266,archive
Katz, D. (2016). Is eastern European "double genocide" revisionism reaching museums? *Dapim: Studies on the Holocaust, 30*(3), 191–220.
Kończal, K. (2020). The invention of the 'cursed soldiers' and its opponents: Post-war partisan struggle in contemporary Poland. *East European Politics and Societies, 34*(1), 67–95.
Kotwas, M., & Kubik, J. (2019). Symbolic thickening of public culture and the rise of right-wing populism in Poland. *East European Politics and Societies, 33*(2), 435–471.
Kowalska-Leder, J. (2023). "Zawołani po imieniu", czyli Krzywda i Sprawiedliwość. *Zagłada Żydów. Studia I Materiały, 18*, 721–759.
Krzywiec, G. (2016). *Chauvinism, Polish style: The case of Roman Dmowski (beginnings: 1886–1905)*. Frankfurt am Main: Peter Lang.
Kucia, M. (2019). The meanings of Auschwitz in Poland, 1945 to the present. *Holocaust Studies, 25*(3), 220–247.
Kukułowicz, T. (2019, January 1). Jakie są gusta muzyczne nastolatków? [What are teenagers' musical tastes?]. *NCK*. Retrieved from https://www.nck.pl/badania/aktualnosci/preferencje-muzyczne-nastolatkow
Kuta, C., & Tęsiorowski, J. (2019). *Obudzić naród do wielkości. Wystąpienia Janusza Kurtyki przez Parlamentem RP 2005–2010 [Awakening the nation to greatness.*

Janusz Kurtyka's speeches before the Parliament of the Republic of Poland 2005–2010]. Warsaw: IPN.

Leszczyński, A. (2020). Furia po rewelacjach o wojennej przeszłości ostatniego "wyklętego". Obelgi i protesty [Fury after revelations about the wartime past of the last 'exiled'. Insults and protests]. Retrieved from https://oko.press/furia-po-rewelacjach-o-wojennej-przeszlosci-ostatniego-wykletego-obelgi-i-protesty

Majewski, P. (2017). Polska dla polaków, nie żaden kurwa ahmed: Analiza narracji islamofobicznych w polskim rapie [Poland for Poles, no for any fucking Ahmed: Analysis of Islamophobia in Polish rap music]. *Kultura Popularna, 3*(53), 111–120.

Majewski, P. (2018). African-American music in the service of white nationalists: Polish "patriotic rap" as a pop cultural tool to promote national values. *European Journal of American Studies, 13*(3), 1–17.

Majewski, P. (2021). *Rap w służbie narodu [Rap in the service of the nation]*. Scholar.

Masters, J., & Mortensen, A. (2018, February 21). 'Polish minister backs call for "Polocaust" museum. *CNN*. Retrieved from https://edition.cnn.com/2018/02/21/europe/poland-minister-backs-polocaust-museum-intl/index.html

Mazur, M. (2022). Rozważania nad historiografią polskiego powojennego podziemia niepodległościowego [Reflections on the historiography of the Polish post-war independence underground]. *Kwartalnik Historyczny, 129*(2), 411–447.

MEN. (2018). *Podstawa programowa kształcenia ogólnego z komentarzem: szkoła podstawowa historia – historia [Core curriculum for general education with commentary: Primary school – history]*. Warsaw: MEN.

MEN. (2022). Rozporządzenie Ministra Edukacji i Nauki z dnia 8 marca 2022 r. [Regulation of the Minister of Education and Science of 8 March 2022]. Dziennik Ustaw, 17 marca 2022 r. Poz. 622.

MEN. (n.d.). Żołnierze niezłomni [Indomitable soldiers]. Retrieved from https://zpe.gov.pl/a/zolnierze-niezlomni/DbQNHeYgG

Ministerstwo Sprawiedliwości. (2018). Narodowy Dzień Pamięci Żołnierzy Wyklętych – hołd niezłomnym bohaterom! National Day of Remembrance of the "Cursed Soldiers" – a tribute to the indomitable heroes!]. Retrieved from https://www.gov.pl/web/sprawiedliwosc/narodowy-dzien-pamieci-olnierzy-wykletych--hold-niezlomnym-bohaterom

Miszczyński, M. (2014). *Hip-hop w Polsce [Hip-hop in Poland]*. Warsaw: WUW.

Mitchell, T. (2001). *Global noise: Rap and hip-hop outside the USA*. Middletown, CT: Wesleyan University Press.

Moroz, A. (2016). *Między pamięcią a historią. Konflikt pamięci zbiorowych Polaków i Białorusinów na przykładzie postaci Rajmunda Rajsa "Burego" [Between memory and history: Conflict of collective memories of Poles and Belarusians on the example of Rajmund Rajs "Bury"]*. Białystok: IPN.

Mosse, G. L. (1988). *Nationalism and sexuality: Middle-class morality and sexual norms in modern Europe*. Madison: University of Wisconsin Press.

Nagel, J. (1998). Masculinity and nationalism: Gender and sexuality in the making of nations. *Ethnic and Racial Studies, 21*(2), 242–269.

Narkowicz, K. (2018). "Refugees not welcome here": State, church and civil society responses to the refugee crisis in Poland. *International Journal of Politics, Culture, and Society, 31*, 357–373.

Narkowicz, K., & Pędziwiatr, K. (2017). Saving and fearing Muslim women in "post-communist" Poland: Troubling Catholic and secular Islamophobia. *Gender, Place and Culture*, *24*(2), 288–299.

Neal, A. M. (1999). *What the music said: Black popular music and black popular culture*. London and New York: Routledge.

Niedźwiedź, A. (2005). *Obraz i postać. Znaczenia wizerunku Matki Boskiej Częstochowskiej [Image and figure: The meanings of the image of the Mother of God of Częstochowa]*. Cracow: WUJ.

Nowicka, E., & Łodziński, S. (2001). *U progu otwartego świata [On the threshold of an open world]*. Cracow: Nomos.

OKO Press. (2020, September 30). Czarnek: Hitler był marksistą [Czarnek: Hitler was a Marxist]. Retrieved from https://oko.press/wypowiedzi/czarnek-hitler-byl-marksista/

Ortner, S. B. (1973). On key symbols. *American Anthropologist*, *75*(5), 1338–1346.

Ostrowska, E. (2004). Matki Polki i ich synowie. Kilka uwag o genezie obrazów kobiecości i męskości w kulturze polskiej [Polish mothers and their sons. Some remarks on the genesis of images of femininity and masculinity in Polish culture]. In M. Radkiewicz (Ed.), *Gender – konteksty [Gender – contexts]* (pp. 215–228). Warsaw: Rabid.

Panfil, T. (2017, September 26). 'Świat Patrzy i Milczy. Sprzeciw Polaków wobec Zła [The world looks on and keeps silent. Poles' opposition to evil]. *Gazeta Polska*. Retrieved from https://www.gazetapolska.pl/14407-swiat-patrzy-i-milczy-sprzeciw-polakow-wobec-zla

Pankowski, R. (2010). Platforma opolska: odcień brunatny' [Platform of Opole in brown colours]. *Nigdy Więcej*, *18*, 3–4.

PAP. (2021, May 19). Kandydat na szefa IPN: Bury brutalizował formy walki z przerażającym wrogiem ojczyzny [Brutalised the forms of struggle against the terrifying enemy of the fatherland]. *Dziennik*. Retrieved from https://wiadomosci.dziennik.pl/historia/aktualnosci/artykuly/8166981,jedwabne-bury-romuald-rajs-karol-nawrocki-ipn.html

Poleszak, S. (2020). Czy okupacyjna przeszłość sierż. Józefa Franczaka "Lalusia" miała wpływ na powojenne losy "ostatniego zbrojnego"? [Did the occupation past of Sgt. Jozef Franczak "Laluś" influence the post-war fate of the "last armed man"?]. *Zagłada Żydów. Studia I Materiały*, *16*, 233–277.

Porter-Szűcs, B. (2014). *Poland in the modern world: Beyond martyrdom*. Hoboken, NJ: Wiley-Blackwell.

Radio Maryja. (2020). Celowe szkalowanie pamięci bohatera J. Franczaka ps. "Laluś". Analiza prawna. [Deliberate slandering of the memory of the hero J. Franczak a.k.a. "Laluś". Legal analysis]. Retrieved from https://www.radiomaryja.pl/informacje/celowe-szkalowanie-pamieci-bohatera-j-franczaka-ps-lalus-analiza-prawna/

RedisBad. (2018). Manifest. Retrieved from https://web.archive.org/web/20170912053511/http://https://www.redisbad.pl/pl/manifest

Rokicki, P. (2015). *Glinciszki i Dubinki. Zbrodnie wojenne na Wileńszczyźnie w połowie 1944 i ich konsekwencje we współczesnych relacjach polsko-litewskich [Glinciszki and Dubinki. War crimes in the Vilnius region in mid-1944 and their consequences in contemporary Polish-Lithuanian relations]*. PAN.

Sejm. (2001). *Sprawozdanie Stenograficzne ze 104 posiedzenia Sejmu Rzeczpospolitej Polskiej w dniach 14 i 15 marca 2001. [Stenographic report on the 104th meeting of the Sejm of the Republic of Poland of 14 and 15 March 2001]*. Warsaw: Sejm.

Sejm. (2006). *Sprawozdanie Stenograficzne ze 14 posiedzenia Sejmu Rzeczpospolitej Polskiej z dnia 14 marca 2006. [Stenographic report on the 14th meeting of the Sejm of the Republic of Poland of 14 March 2006]*. Warsaw: Sejm.

Sejm. (2011). *Sprawozdanie Stenograficzne ze 84 posiedzenia Sejmu Rzeczpospolitej Polskiej z dnia 3 lutego 2006. [Stenographic report on the 84th meeting of the Sejm of the Republic of Poland of 3 February 2011]*. Warsaw: Sejm.

Sejm. (2012). *Sprawozdanie Stenograficzne ze 25 posiedzenia Sejmu Rzeczpospolitej Polskiej z dnia 9 listopada 2012. [Stenographic report on the 84th meeting of the Sejm of the Republic of Poland of 9 November 2012]*. Warsaw: Sejm.

Steinlauf, M. C. (1997). *Bondage to the dead: Poland and the memory of the Holocaust*. Syracuse: Syracuse University Press.

Subotic, J. (2019). *Yellow star, red star: Holocaust remembrance after communism*. Ithaca, NY: Cornell University Press

Theweleit, K. (1987). *Male fantasies*. Minneapolis: University of Minnesota Press.

Turda, M., & Weindling, P. J. (Eds.). (2007). *Blood and homeland: Eugenics and racial nationalism in Central and Southeast Europe, 1900–1940*. Budapest: Central University Press.

Walicki, A. (1994). *Philosophy and romantic nationalism: The case of Poland*. Notre Dame: University of Notre Dame Press.

Yuval-Davis, N. (1997). *Gender & nation*. London: Sage.

Zaremba, M. (2006). *Communism – legitimacy – nationalism*. Frankfurt am Main: Peter Lang.

Żuk, P., & Żuk, P. (2018). Multimodal analysis of the nationalist discourse and historical inspirations of the spectacle of the populist right in Poland between 2015 and 2017. *Discourse Context Media, 26*, 135–143.

5 Heroes? Partisans? Bandits?

The 'Cursed Soldiers' from Below

The meanings and emotions constructed by top-down memory politics cannot be taken for granted. Even if PiS controls the state institutions, incorporates popular culture, and collaborates with the Church to produce a hegemonic collective memory around the key symbol of the 'cursed soldiers', it cannot be assumed that this symbolism reaches a wide audience and that it is interpreted and felt in accordance with its creators' intentions. Hegemonic meanings can always be decoded in different ways, including ways that undermine the hegemonic message (Hall, 1980). Recipients also engage with the message to varying degrees (Morley, 2006; Schrøder, 2000). An opinion poll conducted relatively long ago showed that 58% of respondents know nothing or very little about the PPP (CBOS, 2017). The polls have little to say about such people, lumping them into the 'don't know' or 'hard to say' categories. However, behind these passing answers there may be more complex meanings and emotions that escape when trying to 'measure' them with brief closed-ended standardised questions. Quantitative opinion surveys assume that there is public opinion, i.e. that people have well-defined and consistent views (Bourdieu, 1993; Kilias, 2004). But people's views are often contradictory, fragmented, incoherent, and/or formulated ad hoc in the course of social interaction. Moving beyond such a simplistic quantitative approach, we analyse attitudes that are hidden in opinion polls under the answers 'don't know' or 'hard to say' (Jaskulowski, 2019).

In our research, we therefore included people who are not interested in the topic of the 'cursed soldiers', although they are, willingly or unwillingly, the addressees of this politics, e.g. in passing by murals dedicated to the 'cursed soldiers'. Taking into account the degree of interest and emotional involvement in the theme of the 'cursed soldiers', we distinguished two categories of interviewees, which we conventionally call 'Indifferent' and 'Engaged'. It should be emphasised that the Indifferent were interviewees who had little interest and emotional involvement in memory politics, which, however, says nothing about their attitude to hegemonic politics. They were unintentional recipients of the memory politics, while they did not themselves take the initiative, nor did they seek knowledge about the underground. The Engaged, on

DOI: 10.4324/9781003368847-5
This chapter has been made available under a CC-BY-NC-ND 4.0 license.

the contrary, were interviewees who took a keen interest in the theme of the 'cursed soldiers', who were emotionally moved by it and who sought knowledge about the underground. This does not mean that the Engaged accepted the hegemonic memory politics. Their involvement took various forms; it could manifest itself in support for, and participation in, the commemoration of the 'cursed soldiers', but it could also take the form of criticism of this politics.

The Indifferents

The Indifferents were united not only by their lack of greater interest in the topic of the 'cursed soldiers' but also by the fact that they noticed relatively little of this symbolism in their everyday life. Yet, they were aware of the existence of this memory politics, and some perceived its intensification in recent years. To gain insights into what they thought about this politics, group interviews using audiovisual materials ('cursed soldiers' symbolism, pictures of murals, etc.) were particularly useful as a starting point for discussion (Banks, 2001). Such materials facilitated the interviewees' recollection of various other artefacts or events commemorating the 'cursed soldiers' (e.g. murals in the neighbourhood where they live). The lack of interest in this topic was particularly evident among relatively young people, which may be surprising given the emphasis on this theme in history school education after the right wing took power. This lack of interest translated into little knowledge of the underground itself. The interviewees were familiar with the symbol of the 'cursed soldiers', but some of them did not really know which historical event to relate it to. Some interlocutors said outright that they knew nothing about the underground: 'I have to admit that this is the first time I have ever heard about this topic'. In general, however, most interviewees indicated that the symbol refers to the armed struggle between communists and their opponents immediately after the Second World War, although its genesis was often unclear to them.

The interviewees had some idea of two figures, namely Inka and Pilecki. However, even these two iconic figures were not recognisable to all of them: 'there is one... Pilecki... yes Pilecki was his name... but actually I don't know.... I don't remember'. However, the majority of the interviewees associate the 'cursed soldiers' mainly with these two figures, thus perceiving Pilecki as a partisan in line with the hegemonic narrative. However, these figures, and others that they sometimes mentioned, functioned in their statements not so much as references to specific historical people but as archetypes of some attitudes. What these attitudes were depended on how they assessed the underground as a whole, and most importantly on what their attitude was to the ruling right-wing government. Paradoxically, for example, some interviewees associated Pilecki with 'fascism' and 'Nazis', and Inka with 'anti-Semitism' and 'crimes'. As one interviewee wondered, 'did she murder someone? (...) Or was she not an anti-Semite? (...) some negative things about her...'. For other interviewees they were national heroes who 'fought for an independent Poland'. Thus, the Indifferent knew very little about the underground itself, and their assessment of the underground and their attitude to the symbolism of the 'cursed soldiers' was determined by their political views and their attitude to the right wing, with which they generally associated this symbolism. If an interviewee was anti-right wing, then they simultaneously projected their negative assessment onto the historical symbolism they associated with the right wing.

The Indifferents explained that they were not interested in the underground for various reasons. Some Indifferents were not interested in the past at all and were focused on the present or the future. Younger Indifferents associated the past with monotonous school history, which focused on the military history of Poland, which bored them. The symbolism of the 'cursed soldiers' was part of this experience:

> The war... was the main theme of almost every lesson (...) from primary to secondary school (...) it was just pushed in so hard.... I have cut myself off from it completely and I am not able to listen to it, because it bores me so incredibly.

This sense of boredom was also socially confirmed and reinforced in the course of social interaction, as the interviewee's social environment perceived school history education similarly.

The Indifferents also generally had no family memories related to the underground, and such stories did not circulate in the communicative memory of the various groups to which they belonged. According to them the 'cursed soldiers' were part of the official cultural memory, which they perceived as distant from their everyday life, of little interest and evoking little emotion on a daily basis. Others explained their indifference on the grounds that this theme had become too politicised and had taken on too extreme a form; for example, they were repulsed by the 'primitive masculinity and violence' expressed by this symbolism. Another interviewee clarified that the commemoration has taken the form of some kind of fervent religious devotion, which has a repulsive effect on him: 'I'm just irritated by this whole cult (...) that's why I don't feel like exploring the subject any further (...) because I don't like extremes'. Some older interviewees who had lived in PRL for most of their lives expressed confusion about the memory politics, which they described as 'propaganda' that is not worth being interested in because it changes with the governments. Thus, a pensioner claimed 'I don't know anything anymore', because he was taught at school that 'Dzierżyński was a hero, there were ceremonies, streets, squares... then... tell me... how it is now... was he a hero or not, because (...) they say it this way and that way'.

Although the Indifferents were not interested in memory politics, they were influenced by it. They used, in line with the hegemonic discourse, the term 'cursed soldiers', which they took for granted. In accordance with the hegemonic discourse, most interlocutors repeated that the communists tried to erase the memory of the underground. This is why these soldiers were called the 'cursed'. The Indifferents thus reproduced the ring-wing narrative pattern. However, there were some exceptions: to some Indifferents, the term 'the cursed' was associated negatively, but they found it difficult to say anything more about who had 'cursed' partisans and why: 'they must have done something wrong'. The indifferents also generally reproduced the right-wing narrative that the topic of the draftees only appeared in the public sphere with the coming to power of the right wing: 'when PiS came to power (…) suddenly they took out a story like this …'.

As we have already noted, however, the Indifferent category was not homogeneous but divided into opponents and supporters of the commemoration of the 'cursed soldiers'. One can even see a certain polarisation of attitudes, which may be indicative of the impact of this memory politics, which has an antagonising character and is difficult to ignore, even if the recipient is not interested in the subject. So, on the one hand, there are the Indifferents who have a negative attitude to the commemorations, while, on the other hand, there are interviewees who look approvingly at right-wing politics.

Young people, in particular, who had studied or had a higher education and declared left-wing or liberal views, predominated among the Indifferents who were critical of the symbolism of the 'cursed soldiers'. They looked at this symbolism through the prism of their attitude to the right: 'there's this right-wing, they have their heroes (…) I just put it in a box, that it wasn't like that and that's it, another thing that supports this myth of their... Poland'. They looked at the symbolism not so much as a concept relating to the past but as a right-wing ideological construct that mythologises the past. They emphasised that the 'cursed soldiers' are an element of right-wing memory politics glorifying the allegedly exceptional heroism of Poles. They pointed to the militaristic overtones of this symbol, which fits in with the right-wing need to create an enemy against whom the nation must unite to fight: 'it fits this constant search for an enemy; we the "cursed" are fighting and defending the homeland today against lesbians, refugees, migrants'. From their perspective, the 'cursed soldiers' symbolism is 'such an ideological statement of the right-wing', which builds its support using the sense of threat it creates itself: 'they would always find someone so that there would be a fight for the sake of fighting'.

Some of the Indifferent believed that the symbolism of the 'cursed soldiers' promotes hatred and as such should be banned in public institutions

> I remember at school (…) once a first-grader came in Red is Bad clothes, what the fuck is that, we went to the headmaster (…) we arranged a ban on wearing Red is Bad (…) this is what freedom of speech should look like in my opinion, only for the left....

Others indicated rather that this symbol does not so much express right-wing ideology as it is a reflection of the dominant tendency to construct Polish history as a sequence of wars fought by male heroes. They considered it an archaic remnant at odds with their value system, which focuses on the quality of present and future everyday life.

Indifferent critics of the memory politics paid a lot of attention to the aesthetics of the representations of the 'cursed soldiers'. They viewed these representations through the prism of class stereotypes reproducing social distinctions of good taste (Bourdieu, 1984). In their view, this aesthetic is a manifestation of the inferior taste typical of the uneducated poor lower classes, the subculture of the 'charvers', i.e. residents of block housing estates, who abuse alcohol and are prone to violence, and the rural inhabitants of the 'worst' parts of Poland. As one of the interviewees explained, such people identify themselves with 'the cursed soldiers', compensating for their low social and economic status in the symbolic sphere: 'it's a syndrome that, well, they were oppressed and I am also oppressed, living in a small flat, in a poor family, and this also translates into this'. Wearing patriotic clothing or listening to nationalist rap is, from the Indifferents' point of view, a manifestation of 'cringe' and a sign of belonging to the underclass: 'it's cringe, because of the fact that most often we see in these T-shirts (...) guys who do rioting after getting drunk'. For Indifferents it's an embarrassing and shameful thing, a manifestation of an exotic aesthetic that they very rarely encounter in their everyday life because it exists on the margins of their social world. As one interviewee put it, 'in my bubble no one walks around... no one puts it on...', unless as a joke: 'the strategy to cope with it is to laugh at it'.

At the same time, however, the interviewees treated such commemorations as murals or 'patriotic' clothing as a kind of profanation. Paradoxically, in spite of their irony, they acknowledged that these symbols were somehow important to them. They felt that a building's wall or a T-shirt was not the right place for national symbols because they were too ordinary and exposed these symbols to damage. Interestingly, in a similar vein, there were some radical nationalists who said that clothing with national symbols can only be worn on festive occasions and not for everyday life or a party where we get drunk and 'puke on an eagle, flag or cursed soldier on a hoodie'. The Indifferents habitually treated national symbols as an element of monumental cultural memory that should only be evoked in a specific festive context such as a school academy to celebrate a national holiday: 'it alludes to war themes and (...) for us it is so culturally marked (...) and we approach it with respect (...) and it's kind of distasteful in the face of how we as a nation treat such things'.

The Indifferents also emphasised that the symbol of the 'cursed soldiers' in everyday life functions as an emblem of group membership, i.e. the group of 'charvers' and 'football hooligans'. They emphasised the young age, male gender and psychological basis of group membership related to their immaturity and some kind of complexes: 'some kind of unhealthy models of masculinity (...) it's a bit of an incel thing'. The Indifferents felt that the 'cursed soldiers' in this context act as a sign to identify 'their own' and manifest their belonging to the group, but this is not followed by any interest in the past: 'the motives are simple, I like this band, so I have a T-shirt with the band on it, and the same with the cursed soldiers, (...) these people don't know history (...) they define themselves and it is such an identifying symbol'. The Indifferents emphasised that for such reasons too they are not interested in the 'cursed soldiers', because they do not want to be identified with football hooligans, 'and I want to be away from it, I don't want to have to deal with it, I wish it didn't exist, I would like to cure everyone'. Note that the interviewee pathologises these groups by implicitly contrasting them with 'healthy' society. Some Indifferents, especially younger people, declared that they generally do not identify with any subculture or figure: 'I personally don't have such a character, I rather avoid such situations that someone is 100% perfect, they are my hero (...) an authority, nobody is'. Such declarations can be interpreted as a manifestation of individualisation, at least at the level of self-identification.

The Indifferents were not interested in the past to which 'cursed soldiers' symbolism referred. However, they feel strongly about those who referred to this symbolism, especially in its everyday form. They often spoke of a sense of danger and fear of young men wearing 'patriotic clothes': 'Whenever I see such a T-shirt,... I immediately associate it with aggression...' As another Indifferent said, linking the manifestation of the symbolism of the 'cursed soldiers' with uncontrollable violence, 'they are totally unpredictable people and very often this is linked to drug and alcohol abuse, which only increases the violent behaviour'. The Indifferents were afraid and tried to avoid such people: 'not far from where I live there is a stadium; when there is a match I am afraid to leave the house'.

It is important to note, however, that some Indifferents spoke positively about the commemoration of the 'cursed soldiers' and the underground itself. In accordance with the hegemonic discourse, they saw the 'cursed soldiers' as national heroes. In line with the hegemonic message, they also argued that little had been done to commemorate them after the fall of communism and that they had essentially been allowed to be appropriated by the far right and by football fans. These latter groups were the only ones to cultivate the memory of the underground, which is what influenced these commemorations to take the form they did. The aggressive symbolism and trashy aesthetics are therefore, in their view, partly the 'fault' of mainstream politicians, who gave space to the right wing and football fans. In their view, it was not so much that PiS invented the 'cursed soldiers' but that it took over the symbol from football fans and far-right circles in order to attract more radical voters as part of its populist politics. In their view, this is the strategy of PiS, which presents itself as an advocate of the interests of lower and marginalised social groups.

> I think that this discourse related to the cursed soldiers, that it could be linked with transformation and to those people who were marginalised... they

can feel like these cursed soldiers and today they identify with these values, well, because I have the impression that this is the social group more towards the right, and when it comes to this kind of narrative that is present in politics it is such a political tool (...) that populists use to challenge the elites who took power after 1989....

In their view, the right-wing memory politics is the symbolic equivalent of social programmes, ennobling the marginalised as bearers of the same values as the 'cursed soldiers'. They did not criticise popular representations, considering them to be a kind of naïve art form that cannot be looked down upon: 'Well, someone wears this T-shirt on the street and she just likes this T-shirt (...) then why should it be a cringe?' They also had nothing against commemorating the 'cursed soldiers' in ordinary contexts, because it was consistent with the message that partisans were ordinary people: 'it fits with this narrative to me that the cursed soldiers are one of us'. And some thought it was a good way to promote knowledge of history: 'it's good that they're in pop culture, because then maybe more people will be interested in them'.

It can be said that a certain ambivalence is evident in the attitude of the Indifferents towards the symbolism of the 'cursed soldiers'. On the one hand, this symbol aroused boredom among many Indifferents and a sense of both danger and fear in their everyday lives – due to aggressive bearers of this symbolism, with whom, however, they rarely had to deal because they belonged to a different social world. On the other hand, they included the 'cursed soldiers' in the pantheon of national symbols that should deserve respect. The Indifferents constituted a small proportion of our interviewees, but our sample, according to the logic of qualitative research, is not representative (Strauss & Corbin, 1998). It is therefore not possible to draw any further conclusions, except as a hypothesis. It could be hypothesised that the low number of Indifferents may be due to the fact that the memory politics of 'cursed soldiers' has intensified in recent years, which has led more and more people to take an interest in the PPP. This interpretation is supported by the fact that even among the Indifferents, a certain polarisation can be observed. They felt the need to speak out for or against its commemoration. However, it should be noted that the small number of Indifferents may have been due to the fact that it was mainly those who were interested in the underground who agreed to the interview, who felt that they had knowledge of the subject and that they would be good interviewees. Those who were not interested in it felt that they would not say much, so an interview with them would be pointless.

The Engaged

The Engaged were vividly interested in the PPP and their statements were more 'thick' and detailed than those of the Indifferents. This was linked to the fact that some Engaged had family memories of the underground: their relatives had been active in the underground or had been victims of it. The Engaged were a diverse group in terms of age, education and place of residence. They also had quite diverse views, but certain patterns of argumentation can be discerned. There were two main issues that divided them. First, the attitude towards the term 'cursed soldiers' itself, especially the term 'cursed'. The interviewees saw the term as questionable and contentious. Thus, in contrast to the Indifferents, they emphasised that the very name is already a subject of political dispute. Second, the interviewees had different attitudes towards the underground itself and, consequently, also towards the right-wing memory politics. A polarisation can be observed among the Engaged, so that interviewees either criticised the memory politics or were in favour of it, which some of them actually co-created and implemented. The different assessments were also accompanied by different emotional reactions, ranging from pride or respect to fear, a sense of threat or anger.

Taking these two criteria, we get a total of four categories of Engaged, which we conventionally call 'Apologists', 'Allies', 'Critics', and 'Outsiders'. The Apologists accepted the very notion of 'cursed soldiers' and evaluated the underground positively, which also implied a positive attitude towards the hegemonic memory politics. This also translated into what emotions they experienced: pride, respect but also shame, as we will see. The Allies rejected the notion of the 'cursed soldiers' but assessed the underground positively and this mainly evoked emotions of pride and respect, and to some extent a kind of weariness. The Critics rejected the term 'cursed soldiers', assessed the underground negatively, and opposed its commemoration in the current form. Here we very often had to deal with fear, a sense of threat and anger. Finally, for the Outsiders, who accepted the notion but evaluated the underground negatively and rejected the hegemonic memory politics, the dominant emotion was irony, but interviewees also spoke of fear or a sense of marginalisation.

The Apologists

Apologists were a heterogeneous group in terms of socio-demographic characteristics – it is difficult to identify any clear patterns here. They accepted the term 'cursed soldiers' as adequately describing the post-war partisans. In their statements, one can see a similar paradox to that of the history teachers we interviewed, who believed that history is an objective science, while at the same time emphasising that history is supposed to teach that the nation is the highest value. There was no contradiction here, because in teachers' social world nations are not contingent constructs but fundamental social entities given by nature or god. An individual in their view is by nature a member of a nation to which they have a 'natural' moral duty of loyalty (Jaskulowski et al., 2022). Apologists tended to combine two seemingly contradictory theses: that the term 'the cursed soldiers' objectively describes the past – 'they were cursed... these are the facts' – while at the same time stating that the

Heroes? Partisans? Bandits? The 'Cursed Soldiers' from Below 75

use of this term is a certain ideological choice. Similarly to the teachers, the Apologists saw their ideological interpretation of the past not just as a political construct but as a reality per se.

Although the Apologists following the hegemonic memory politics accepted the term 'cursed soldiers', they interpreted the word 'cursed' in various ways. Basically, all of them, in line with the hegemonic discourse, reproduced the thesis that the communists had a deliberate politics of forgetting. The reproduction of the hegemonic discourse was interspersed with memories of family members who were partisans and were repressed: 'in my grandmother's family, there was a cousin who was in the AK, he disclosed himself, ended up in the UB, but just magically committed suicide'. Apologists here spoke of a 'conspiracy of silence', indicating that in the official public sphere in the PRL the issue of post-war partisanship was taboo, while in the private sphere it was talked about reluctantly, fearing negative consequences. Fear appeared in the accounts of the interviewees, but as a memory of their parents or grandparents, rather than as an emotion experienced today. Some said that they only learned about such family stories in the early 1990s, when it ceased to be a taboo subject and parents or grandparents became more willing to talk about it.

Apologists, however, had a different opinion as to whether the term 'cursed soldiers' describes the memory politics well after 1989. Some reproduced the hegemonic narrative by claiming that the III RP continued the communist politics and only the PiS government broke with it. Others believed that PiS itself was initially not interested in commemoration either, which only a small group of radical nationalists did. From the perspective of radical nationalists, the official memory politics is a 'stolen tradition', which PiS instrumentally uses to mobilise more radical voters, even though it has done little itself to cultivate the memory of the 'cursed soldiers'. Interestingly, some radical nationalists have strongly emphasised that it was not only the communists who 'cursed' the partisans but also the Catholic Church. This may seem surprising, since radical nationalists emphasised the links between Polishness and Catholicism. Yet, at the same time they are critical of the contemporary Church, which is too liberal and left-wing, and some believe it has been controlled by the homosexual-paedophile lobby.

Some Apologists rejected the hegemonic message, arguing that the III RP had already begun to restore the memory of the PPP, so it cannot be said that the partisans were 'cursed' after 1989. As they claimed, such theses are a reproduction of the PiS's propaganda, which seeks to present itself as the only truly Polish party. They indicated that it was necessary to emphasise the role of the III RP in developing the memory politics of 'cursed soldiers' in order to refute the PiS's arguments that it is the only party that cares about national memory. Apologists, in line with the logic of hegemonic discourse, used the term 'curse soldiers' in a confrontational manner as a kind of accusation against their opponents. To a certain extent, the differences among the interviewees mirror the conflicts between the supporters of the centrist and right-wing parties and are also a reflection of the sort of game of nationalism dominating the public space in Poland. The parties compete with each other as to which of them best represents the Polish national interest and is the best guardian of national memory, which is also evident in the statements of our interviewees (Jaskulowski & Kilias, 2016).

It must be stressed that the Apologists identified with a variety of political options and cannot be identified only with supporters of the right. However, there was a predominance of right-wing and centre-right supporters, with almost no left-wing interlocutors. There were some differences between supporters of different political options. Apologists with centrist political sympathies tended to understand the symbolism of the 'cursed soldiers', metaphorically speaking, in a thin way. They attributed rather general meaning to this symbol, such as independence or the Polish nation-state, without specifying it in more detail. In accordance with the logic of hegemonic discourse, they placed the 'cursed soldiers' in the line of other national heroes such as the January insurgents or the Warsaw insurgents, who fought for an independent Polish state, but did not explain in detail how this state was to be structured (Cohen, 1985). Their statements show a tendency to externalise communism as something alien to Poles, but they did not give it any clear ethnic meaning. They saw this symbol primarily as uniting Poles, and so its meaning had to be quite vague in order to be accepted by every Pole just like the figure of the Warsaw insurgent, the emblem, or the flag:

> there is no doubt at all that we should all cherish the memory of the Warsaw insurgents, although… there are disputes about whether the uprising was right or wrong (…) so… likewise the memory of the cursed soldiers (…) it belongs to all Poles.

Interviewees declaring right-wing views, however, defined the symbol of the 'cursed soldiers' in a way that was, metaphorically speaking, 'dense' and more in line with the right-wing project. In a word, the 'cursed soldiers' represented not simply a fight for an independent Poland but a fight for a very specific Poland. Thus, according to this understanding, the 'cursed soldiers' symbolised the conservative Catholic ethnic Polish nation-state. These Apologists attributed a whole set of meanings to the symbol of the 'cursed soldiers' based on the principle of 'all or nothing' reproducing the hegemonic logic of the key symbol that evokes the whole right-wing mythical-symbolic complex. The tendency to externalise communism was also strongly evident in their statements, which is why they objected to referring to the 'civil war' in post-war Poland as communism was mainly introduced by the Russians – as they claimed. Some also invoked the myth of Judeo-Communism, claiming that Jews controlled the security service, and referred to various conspiracy theories suggesting that, for example, the communists themselves organised pogroms against Jews in post-war Poland in order to discredit the PPP. Following the logic of the hegemonic memory discourse, they also emphasised the role of other allegedly 'communised' national minorities such as Belarusians. At the same time, they marginalised the role of Polish communists by excluding them from the Polish nation as 'traitors' or 'social margins'. As one interviewee said, 'if someone was a commie by choice, he was a commie, not a Pole'.

Some radical right-wing Apologists also tended towards a kind of genealogical interpretation of contemporary Polish politics. They framed the political conflict as a struggle between the 'grandchildren of the cursed soldiers' and the 'third generation of the UB', a reflection of right-wing journalism that uses similar rhetoric. They emphasised that the opponents of the commemoration of 'cursed soldiers' are descendants of UB functionaries and now occupy various privileged positions in society. This fits in with the populist rhetoric of the right wing about the post-communist system ruling Poland after 1989, in which the key role was played by former communist elites allied with the liberal opposition. Given the tendency to externalise communism, the phrase 'third generation of the UB' also contains a suggestion of the non-Polish origins. However, interviewees rarely express it explicitly. Some employees of memory politics institutions sometimes used allusive language, saying, for example, the 'proper' or 'real' names of various communist activists. There were, however, exceptions, to mention one interviewee associated with a major memory institution who suggested that leading SLD and PO politicians were 'Jews'. Some interviewees put it directly: 'Kwasniewski, many of them changed their names to Polish'.

The Apologists shared the conviction that anti-communist partisans were unambiguous national heroes who should be revered: 'they are heroes, the greatest heroes'. They emphasised that the accomplishments of the 'cursed soldiers' aroused pride and admiration in them. Apologists also felt gratitude because they believed, in line with the hegemonic message, that without the sacrifice of the partisans, the communists would have 'completely communised Poland'. Their resistance made the communists realise that Polish society did not accept Soviet domination, which dampened their politics. As one interviewee put it briefly, 'thanks to the cursed soldiers we still speak Polish'. In addition, the memory of their sacrifice was cultivated in the family sphere and served as an inspiration for later oppositionists, especially Solidarity, which would not have come into being if there had not been the 'cursed soldiers' before. These statements fit into the canonical and dominant narrative about Polish uprisings, which, although they generally ended in defeat, kept the 'spirit' of resistance alive among Poles (Jaskulowski et al., 2022). Regardless of their political views, the Apologists perceived the 'cursed soldiers' as heroes deserving of a place in the national pantheon. In this context, Apologists reproduced the hegemonic discourse and deny or marginalise the crimes of the underground.

The interviewees here referred to several strategies. The first strategy can be described as 'deserved punishment'. The interviewees justified the murders of the local population on the grounds that they supported the communists militarily: 'this Belarusian population was not just ordinary mothers, looking after their children, loving fathers. No – they were armed ... communists (...) but there is this media narrative – "oh, these poor Belarusians ... Bury shot them"'. Others argued that the murder of Jews was understandable revenge for the alleged fact that Jews collaborated with the communists in 1939 when the Soviet Union sneakily attacked Poland. Interviewees here reproduced a hegemonic discourse showing a tendency to externalise communism, which was particularly evident among those interviewees with right-wing views. Some right-wing interviewees echoed the stereotype of Judeo-Communism or that of the Belarusian-Communist. At the same time, the interlocutors denied that the 'cursed soldiers' murdered Jews as Jews or Belarusians as Belarusians. They framed the murders not as crimes motivated by national hatred but as part of the national liberation struggle against communism. Jews or Belarusians died at the hands of the underground as security service functionaries, not as persons of other nationalities. Paradoxically, they denied having prejudices against other nations, while evoking negative stereotypes about them.

Another strategy is to deny the crimes in general and frame them as baseless accusations: 'they talk about Bury (...) they say that he killed people somewhere in Belarus (...) that he killed children. No. None of them did that. It was just a fight for ... to overthrow this government'. Another interviewee, an employee of a memory institution, when discussing the partisans' attitude towards civilians, changed the subject by resorting to a defensive reaction: 'there is already such a paranoia that it is the Poles who are, as it were, to blame for starting the Second World War, (...) this is still emerging and I think that in a few decades (...) such a narrative will be dominant'. The interviewee framed the conversation about the crimes of the underground within the framework of an international slander campaign allegedly being waged against Poland – a reflection of the hegemonic right-wing discourse, which, as we have seen, uses a rhetoric of suspicion, suggesting the existence of some conspiracy to destroy Poland's good image. In this context, there was a feeling of shame located at both the collective and individual level. The interviewees felt responsible for Poland's good image and felt a kind of shame that they were not doing enough to give resistance to these 'slanders' that might cling to Poland and cause their compatriots to be ashamed of being Polish.

The third strategy was to adopt a normative definition of the 'cursed soldiers'. Thus, one interviewee explained that his grandparents had told him very bad things about the partisans, that they robbed and killed people for no reason. The interviewee, however, rejected such stories: 'but I'd make a big distinction (...) the cursed soldiers were really great people (...) also I heard more... de facto not about the cursed soldiers, but about such groups robbing villages'. According to this normative approach, a 'cursed soldier' could not commit a crime, because then they ceased to be a 'cursed soldier' and became a bandit. This mode of argumentation is a variation of a discursive mechanism present in the Polish public sphere: if Poles commit crimes they are symbolically excluded from the Polish nation as a social margin, degenerates, deviants who do not represent true Polishness. Similarly, a Polish soldier who commits crimes ceases to be a Polish soldier and becomes a criminal (Dobrosielski, 2017).

Another strategy was that the interviewees appealed to higher necessity: 'they only look at these crimes, alleged crimes (...) and they do not look at the deeper meaning of these actions'. As another interviewee explained, 'they robbed out of necessity (...) probably often they had to exploit that population somewhere, but with a heavy heart'. The interviewee notes that those who protest against the commemoration do not realise that the fight for independence required various resources, which the partisans lacked and had to acquire by force, but are justified by their noble goal. They referred here to various historical examples, e.g. the AK, which no one accuses of requisitioning food or liquidating traitors who threatened their security. This mode of argumentation reflects a rather typical feature of nationalist discourse, which has the power to legitimise various actions, even those that people generally describe as criminal, as long as they can be given a national sanction.

The next strategy was typical of interviewees declaring radically right-wing views and can be described as realistic. This strategy was often accompanied by other strategies. Here, the interviewees sometimes referred to a book by the right-wing publicist Piotr Zychowicz (2018), *Skazy na pancerzach* (Flaws on Armour), which caused an outcry in right-wing circles because it argued that history cannot be idealised and showed that the 'cursed soldiers' committed crimes. However, for the interviewees, although the 'cursed soldiers' had flaws, they were still 'knights' of sorts as suggested by the title of the book. The interviewees presented themselves as realists accepting the world as it is in reality, not in idealistic imaginations. They relativised the crimes of the 'cursed soldiers' by appealing to a kind of Realpolitik: 'Bury, for example, did the pacification there (...) but he didn't do (...) out of hatred for them, no? They just had some of their orders there, plans'. As they explained, the post-war reality was governed by its own laws; violence was an everyday occurrence at the time and was an accepted way of resolving conflicts. One cannot, they argued, judge the 'cursed soldiers' through the prism of the standards of our times. The partisans operated under pressure and sometimes they did things they perhaps should not have done, but what they did was within the standards of the era. Their critics exaggerate the crimes of the 'cursed soldiers' and do not take into account the specifics of the times. It is necessary to approach reality realistically: the 'cursed soldiers' lived in difficult times and even if they committed crimes they are national heroes who should be remembered and respected.

The last strategy was simply to avoid the topic. Some interviewees simply cut off the conversation about the crimes: 'I think that here we should maybe keep silent about certain things'. The interlocutors not only expressed their personal position but believed that the official memory politics should celebrate the partisans as moral exemplars and not look for various dark sides in their activities, as this does not serve the interest of the Polish state.

The Allies

Another category of interviewees was Allies who considered the notion of the 'cursed soldiers' to be inadequate, which apparently put them in the position of an oppositional reading. However, the Allies are, in a sense, a subset of the Apologists, as they largely supported the hegemonic politics. Yet, they had doubts about the notion of the 'cursed soldiers'. The division between Apologists and Allies is a reflection of the disagreements within the hegemonic politics as to how to refer to the underground. Although the hegemonic discourse is clearly dominated by the notion of the 'cursed soldiers', the notion of 'the indomitable soldiers' sometimes appears within it – of which the Allies were the very advocates. The Allied group was relatively small, and the vast majority of interviewees sympathetic to the hegemonic politics used the term 'cursed soldiers'. From the point of view of those in favour of the nomenclature of the 'cursed soldiers', especially those who thought in terms of Realpolitik, the term 'indomitable soldiers' is mythology: 'they were soldiers who had various ethical and moral dilemmas, there were good people and bad people, that's why I'm not going to say indomitable, because it's already such a mythology'. An employee of one of the memory institutions referred to another argument, defending the term 'cursed soldiers'. He argued that the term 'indomitable' is, on the one hand, a broader term than 'cursed', but on the other hand, it is narrower and not suitable to describe the 'anticommunist uprising' in post-war Poland. As he explained, the term 'indomitable' is broader because it encompasses all those who fought for a free Poland in different historical eras, so for example the November and January insurgents. However, it is narrower because it includes only those who did not surrender and fought to the end. The term 'cursed soldiers', as opposed to the term 'indomitable soldiers', makes it possible to include also those partisans who were not indomitable to the end and, for example, surrendered or took advantage of the amnesty.

The Allies criticised this way of thinking and argued that indomitability cannot be understood in such zero-one terms, but as a certain attitude and the fact of taking up a fight. The fact that a partisan took advantage of the amnesty does not mean that they were not steadfast – besides, it is not for us to judge, because we live in peaceful conditions and have no idea of war. The Allies criticised the term 'cursed soldiers' as inadequate and advocated consistent use of the term 'indomitable soldiers'. The main argument of the Allies in favour of using the term 'indomitable soldiers' is well reflected in the statement of one interviewee: 'I think I also like this term indomitable soldiers better. Because it defines more their attitude and not what was done to their memory later on'. The interviewee rejects the term 'cursed soldiers' because, in his opinion, it diverts attention away from the partisans themselves and towards the attitude that successive governments had towards them. The notion of 'cursed soldiers' constructs the partisans as a passive object of the memory politics, because partisans are defined in terms of what the communists did with their memory. In general, this notion does not emphasise the qualities of the partisans themselves, such as heroism or sacrifice. For this reason, the Allies preferred the term 'indomitable soldiers' because it strongly emphasised the dispositions of the partisans themselves.

Allies, however, were not a homogeneous category and differed in what meaning they attributed to the symbolism of the 'indomitable soldiers'. Some attributed a thick meaning to this symbolism in line with the ideology of PiS – the underground represented a fight not so much for independence but for a concrete independent Polish state in line with the right-wing project. It was not simply a symbol of an independent Polish state but of a state guaranteeing the dominance of ethnic Poles, Catholicism, and conservative social norms. These interviewees also strongly emphasised that indomitability must also be understood as a certain internal process: a struggle with one's weaknesses, as the partisans resisted the internal and natural temptation to leave the forest, give up fighting and try to live a normal life. Even if they eventually succumbed to this temptation it is not for us to judge. They also strongly emphasised the religiosity of the partisans: their attachment to Catholicism was supposed to give them inner strength.

Others understood the symbolism of 'indomitable soldiers' in a thinly veiled way, so for them this symbol mainly represented the fight for Poland's independence, but without specifying for which Poland. These Allies also put forward an additional argument against the term 'cursed soldiers'. They claimed that the term 'indomitable' was more descriptive and not so clearly associated with one political option: 'I think the most fair and least value-laden term is indomitable'. For this reason, they rejected the term 'cursed soldiers' because it invites the question of who cursed them and entangles the commemoration in political disputes. Thus, in their opinion, such symbols as 'indomitable' soldiers, like, for example, the symbol of the Warsaw Uprising, should unite and not divide Poles, because they symbolise values that every Pole should cherish, namely a sovereign Polish state. Allies accepted the hegemonic message in this respect, which portrayed partisans as national heroes fighting for national freedom. But they preferred other terms that they considered more neutral – usually 'indomitable soldiers'.

The Critics

Critics rejected the hegemonic construction of the underground as 'cursed soldiers' or 'indomitable soldiers'. The critics were a diverse group in terms of age, education, and place of residence, but to some extent they were united by their political views. Most had left-wing or centrist views, although there were also interviewees with conservative-liberal beliefs, but who were critical of the ruling right. Critics can also include the majority of Belarusian interviewees. Among the Critics, especially those declaring themselves as Belarusians, there were interlocutors who had various family traumatic memories related to the underground or knew such stories circulating in the communicative memory of their local communities. Their interest and emotional involvement thus stemmed from personal experiences that conflicted with the official message.

Critics saw in the symbol of the 'cursed soldiers' a condensed representation of the right-wing ideology identified with PiS. They viewed this symbol through a thick definition. They believed that the symbol was invented and appropriated by PiS, which gave it a specific meaning in line with its political ideology. In their view, the symbol of the 'cursed soldiers' cannot be seen as yet another national symbol such as the flag or the emblem, both of which simply represent the Polish nation-state and are open to different interpretations. In contrast to these symbols, 'cursed soldiers' has specifically right-wing undertones. As one interviewee put it, 'cursed soldiers' has become a 'tribal totem' so closely associated with PiS that they cannot be separated from each other. It represents only a part of Polish society, which nevertheless pretends to be the true Polish nation. Through this lens, the interviewee continues, the symbolism of the 'cursed soldiers' constitutes the 'founding myth' of the semi-authoritarian nationalist state being built by PiS.

Critics rejected right-wing ideology represented by the symbol of the 'cursed soldiers'. For example, they indicated that the symbol of the 'cursed soldiers' promotes blind heroism as a condition for being a 'true' Pole: 'I dislike terribly this kind of martyrdom, this very cult of sacrificing everything only (...) as if it were the most important thing, the glorification of this whole struggle'. Others denounced the patriarchal masculinity propagated by it, which in their view was an expression of an infantile longing to be a real man. Let us quote a female critic who, as a young student in the 1990s, was part of the right-wing circles:

> I used to get tangled up in the local opposition milieu and I remember that climate (...) they were recalling the past from the 1980s (...) they were right wing, they were so cursed, everything drowned in vodka, yes, they drank it by the litres (...) they must have felt some kind of agitation (...) the sexual climate was crackling (...) we were those brave lads (...) I felt so terrible then... We were young students, they had to show off, they

were older people than us, (...) I remember that Łupaszka was in the top spot then.

The interviewee suggests that the current memory politics focused on the 'cursed soldier' has deeper psychological roots, which have to be sought in male sexual frustrations. Critics rejected the type of attachment to the nation represented by the symbol: 'You can only be a Pole if you have ultra-right-wing views, hate other minorities, want Poland to be white, Catholic, women subjugated' (...) such a narrative about these cursed soldiers (...) for me, Polishness is something different.

Two themes dominated the Critics' statements on the 'cursed soldiers' as a historical symbol. The Critics denounced the instrumental use of history by PiS and the historical falseness of the term 'cursed soldiers'. They emphasised the instrumental use of the symbolism by PiS for the current political struggle. They stated that 'cursed soldiers' is not so much a descriptive as an ideologised term, which aims not to commemorate partisans but to promote party interests. PiS uses the history of the PPP to present itself as the only continuator of patriotic traditions: 'This is an absolutely political aim (...) is to benefit the government'. The party portrays itself as the heir to the insurgent tradition by inscribing the 'cursed soldiers' into the sequence of national liberation struggles culminating in the PiS government. It depicts itself as taking part in the same 'eternal' struggle against Poland's enemies as previous generations of 'insurgents':

> they are building this national identity in opposition to something (...) here were the cursed soldiers (...) now we cannot let Poland, I don't know, lose Christian values (...) only we, Poles, will fight for these Christian values, for this family, as if all of this is endangered (...) it... brings tangible benefits to the ruling party, because people see a sense of danger and at the same time a saviour is pointed out to them.

Critics also indicated that the terms 'cursed soldiers' and 'indomitable soldiers' are a distortion of historical reality. In general, the Critics felt that the underground was too complex a phenomenon to be defined by one single term, while in addition containing such a strong emotional charge. As one interviewee says, for example, for him the partisans were not so much 'indomitable' as devoid of political realism: 'in these IPN discourses, these qualities are mentioned, such as determination, but for me it is (...) lack of a sober view of the situation (...) nationalism, aversion to others, whether these others were Jews, Byelorussians'.

It is also difficult to call the partisans 'soldiers' because there was no army and the AK had been disbanded. They also stressed that this is an ahistorical notion: 'I ask myself whether Pilecki knew he was cursed'. Some interlocutors said that the term 'cursed' is misleading, because during the communist period the topic of the underground appeared in various forms in literature and film and was not eradicated from memory in the III RP. Some interviewees in this context recalled the communist militaristic memory politics and argued that the PPP appeared in communist propaganda as villains, and now the right wing is making heroes out of them, casting communists as villains. Paradoxically, the right wing is declaratively breaking with the communist legacy at the same time as reinstating communist propaganda schemes. Still others rejected the term 'cursed' because, in their view, it falsely implied that the fate of the partisans was determined, that some kind of fate was upon them and they had no choice but to fight and die. They argued that, after all, there were various other options. Many partisans revealed themselves and returned to civilian life, while the vast majority of people did not go into the forest at all. Referring to partisans as the 'cursed' is a projection of right-wing ideology glorifying uncompromising anti-communism and marginalising involvement in rebuilding the country after the war.

Critics have stressed that the symbolism of the 'cursed soldiers' simplifies the complex post-war reality, and that inscribing their battles in the sequence of Polish national uprisings is an abuse. Two strategies were evident here. First, Critics did not agree with the Manichean vision of the post-war reality saying that there were 'good' anti-communists on one side and only 'bad' communists on the other. Critics underlined that after the years of war, people wanted to live normally and rebuild the country. Following the logic of nationalism, Critics believed that a sovereign nation-state was a cherished value and argued that although the PRL was dependent on the Soviet Union, it was a Polish state. They assumed that some communists, not to mention people who simply wanted a return to normal life, joined in the rebuilding of the country and acted from patriotic motives. Moreover, there were other forms of resistance to communism such as Mikołajczyk's PSL. Some referred to family memories in this context:

> my grandmother's uncle (...) was a militiaman and then a member of the Sejm after the war (...) we tend to forget that for the majority (...) returning to the status quo from before the war was not an option. My family (...) were peasants and the Second Polish Republic didn't give them much, I mean, illiteracy in the countryside was over 50%, the farms were small (...) people like my uncle saw in the new system a chance to improve their lives (...) in the Second Polish Republic it would hardly have been possible for a peasant son to be an MP.

The hegemonic discourse idealises the Second Republic as a Polish nation-state 'recovered' after centuries of partition. However, the interviewee emphasised the socially exclusionary nature of this state and that many people saw communism as an opportunity for social advancement.

Second, Critics pointed to the very nature of the underground, which conflicted with its image in hegemonic politics. In their view, the PPP was divided, it did not have a single goal, and partisans often lacked political awareness. They argued that the partisans were mainly young men, generally without any education, who did not so much want to fight for Poland as seek adventure: 'many of them were looking for something they hadn't experienced during the war (...) some adventure, some fulfilment, some male initiation (...) often because they wanted to impress someone in the village, I don't know... a father, a girlfriend'. The Critics stressed the mechanisms that caused partisans to quickly turn into bandits. Thus, the crimes committed by Bury or Łupaszka were not exceptions or some random 'accidents' but resulted from the conditions in which the underground functioned:

> killing, murdering even a civilian person was a tool of struggle and a tool of survival (...) such situations, of which we today accuse Łupaszko or Bury... there were hundreds. Because this was the usual mechanism of that terrible fight (...) this mentality (...) must be called gigantic demoralisation (...). Whereas in our imagination these are partisans sitting around a campfire singing partisan songs and sniffing spruce smoke from a spruce tree.

This picture of a demoralised underground was repeated in the statements of many Critics and was clearly dominant. Some Critics pointed to situational factors such as, for example, the prolonged war or the lowering of the value of human life, which caused partisans hiding in the forests to quickly become bandits. Other Critics more strongly emphasised internal factors, i.e. the views of partisans themselves, particularly those that belonged to ethno-authoritarian nationalist organisations, which pushed them into various criminal actions, especially against national minorities. As one interviewee put it briefly, 'the history of the cursed soldiers is largely a history of violence', which stemmed from their belief that 'national minorities were their natural enemies'.

Interviewees belonging to the middle and older generation recalled family stories circulating in communicative memory in their immediate family. They filtered the hegemonic message through the oral accounts of their relatives, which contradicted the hegemonic narratives of the heroic 'cursed soldiers', who always acted according to the idealised ethos of the Polish soldier. They sought confirmation of their negative image of the underground by reading various critical publications on the underground. Younger critics referred less frequently to family stories and more often drew their knowledge of the PPP from the media, especially social media, and from school. It should be added that in the Polish education system the teacher has relative freedom and space to critically discuss, for example, the content of a textbook. Thus, despite the fact that the PiS reforms have strengthened the nationalist model of education, there are teachers in schools who teach in ways that challenge the dominant narratives, for example, using their own adapted teaching materials (Jaskulowski et al., 2022).

The interviewees cited various stories reporting the violence and cruelty of the partisans, to which, on the basis of the I-witnessing strategy, they gave a privileged status in relation to the hegemonic narratives (Geertz, 1988). Thus, one interviewee recounts a story transmitted within his circle of relatives:

> the guys come out of the forest and what they do to the locals... father, grandfather of a person very close to me (...) they cut off his tongue....
> - tongue... for what?
> I don't know, he didn't give horses, food... he was saying something... (...) I know such accounts (...) post-war stories (...), they come across somewhere, because someone became a school director, it was 1945 they came across and executed him in front of the children, because it was collaboration with the hostile Bolshevik regime, and the guy just took up a job as a school director, he wanted the return of education.

Critics did not treat such stories as isolated cases, rather they tended to see them as significant events, indicative of the degeneration of the underground.

Such stories passed on in the family resonated with fear, which was revived years later with the hegemonic glorification of the partisans. For example, one of the interlocutors recalls the story of his grandmother:

> My grandmother is from a village (...) there was a group of Aleksander Młyński, pseudonym Drągal (...). They often appeared in the neighbouring villages, and, well, here they robbed the local food store (...). And my grandmother very often tells a story about when she was a child (...) and her duties included herding cows (...). Three soldiers from Drągal wanted to take this cow away from her. She hid in a ditch (...) she remembered that she was terribly scared, well (...) there were other stories – they sometimes went at night (...) they entered cottages to get various things, and one such night they entered the cottage, beat up, beat up my grandmother's father, that is my great-grandfather, took his shoes, the last shoes, and left.

The memory politics evokes again these traumatic experiences from the post-war era. The tragic family stories are also overlaid here with a misunderstanding of why bandits are being put on a pedestal who fought against a state that provided social advancement:

> a few years ago (...) the city council wanted to name a street after Drągal. And this evoked an extremely emotional reaction in my grandmother (...) there were also state ceremonies (...) on the anniversary of Drągal's death (...) that he continued the fight against the Sovietisation of Poland (...) but what this means for a woman who has an education, you know, a vocational one, and grew up in a village that was terrorised by this guy.

However, while interviewees spoke of the fear felt by older family members who had directly witnessed post-war crimes, they themselves did not describe their experiences in terms of fear. Rather, they felt anger at the one-sidedness of a hegemonic memory politics that ignores the experiences of people like his grandmother, which do not lend themselves to a militarised and masculinised vision of heroism.

Belarusian Critics

The Belarusian Critics, the vast majority of whom lived in the aforementioned Podlasie, which was one of the PPP's main areas of activity, deserve separate attention. After the establishment of the modern Polish nation-state, the Belarusian ethnic area was divided between Poland and the Soviet Union under the 1921 Riga Treaty. According to the 1931 Polish census, Poland was inhabited by approximately one million Belarusians. Belarusians were generally a rural population, with a low social and economic status, who were also politically marginalised and subjected to assimilation pressures in the Second Republic. The Polish authorities assumed that the Belarusians could be easily assimilated and sought to limit the national activity of the Belarusians, which they viewed in anti-state terms. By the outbreak of the Second World War, almost all of the already sparse Belorussian-language schools had been closed, a process of colonisation of ethnic Belorussian lands by Polish military settlers had been carried out, and the independence of the Orthodox Church, which had become an instrument of Polonisation through the introduction of Polish into liturgy and sermons, had been limited (Kamusella, 2009).

After the Second World War, only a small proportion of Belarusians remained within the new Polish borders, mainly living in the Białystok area, i.e. the south-eastern part of today's Podlaskie Voivodeship. Although declaratively the Polish communists proclaimed an internationalist ideology, in practice, their actions were aimed at creating an ethnically homogeneous Polish state. Thus, by virtue of an agreement between the Polish and Soviet communists, a population exchange was to take place: Belarusians from Poland were to settle in the Soviet Union, from where Poles were to migrate to Poland. The communists claimed that the resettlement was voluntary, but they actually exerted pressure and also imposed forced migration to the Soviet Union. By the end of 1946, around 36,000 people of Belarusian nationality had left the Białystok voivodeship, and 125,000 remained; 80% of the Belarusians did not take the opportunity to resettle in Soviet territory. From this group come representatives of the current Belarusian minority in Poland. According to the 2011 national census, Podlaskie Voivodeship was inhabited by 1,188,300 people, of whom almost 39,000 declared Belarusian nationality. Most Belarusians belong to the Polish Autocephalous Orthodox Church, 76.6% of whose adherents – according to the 2011 census – reside in Podlaskie Voivodeship (Czykwin, 2000).

The memory politics of the 'cursed soldiers' in Podlasie clearly comes into conflict with local memory, or in this case Belarusian 'counter-memory' (Foucault, 1977). Belarusian counter-memory is the memory of a defensive minority that focuses on a sense of injustice, presenting the perspective of the victims of the underground. The interviewees did not want to build a Belarusian identity on a sense of injustice, but the politics of glorifying the 'cursed soldiers' forced them to do so:

> as a group of young Belarusian activists and historians at that time [in the 1980s and 1990s], we did not at all intend to build our historical memory on injustice. We wanted to build on what unites us with the Poles, but we were forced to remember it after all.

In this Belarusian memory, the PPP functioned as a deadly threat. Some interviewees quoted stories of older people who recalled that the real war started in Podlasie only after the Second World War with the activities of anti-communist partisans:

> when I was 18 years old (...) I was talking to an elderly man and he said that the war broke out in 1945, – "What do you mean? (...) 1939 was the war". You know... we didn't even notice anything (...) there were some Germans, then the Soviets, we were living normally (...) the war started in 1945 (...) when the neighbours [Catholic Poles] started coming to us, first they started scaring us, then they stole, and finally they killed us.

According to this story, neither the Soviet occupation nor the German occupation (then Soviet again) brought major changes in the everyday life of Podlasie Belarusians. It was only in the post-war period, due to the activities of the PPP against the Belarusian and Orthodox population, that violence became part of everyday life. A constant element in the stories of the Belarusian interlocutors was the crimes committed by partisans, who were sometimes their Polish and Catholic neighbours, which translated into fear of their neighbours, which caused the witnesses to be not only afraid to talk about it in public for years but also reluctant to talk about it in the closest family circle. However, despite the fear, stories about the crimes circulated in the communicative memory of various Belarusian communities. Over time, the second and third generation of victims began to inquire more boldly about the crimes from their parents and grandparents and to speak openly about it in public. Many interviewees recalled traumatic family histories:

> My grandfather and my grandmother (...) there are two versions, one version says probably, accidentally, and the other one says absolutely not accidentally, they were killed by such a unit, the armed underground,

which is called a band. I recently talked to a villager (...) he used the term AK, although it is not at all certain that they were from AK.

Even today, some interviewees do not know what exactly happened to their relatives and who murdered them. They have a sense of injustice because the state institutions do not try to investigate the circumstances of the various crimes and the 'official' historians of the IPN ignore the subject.

While the hegemonic discourse externalises communism by identifying it with minorities, the Belarusian interviewees point to the participation of Poles in it. They emphasise that Belarusians took jobs in the state administration because of the opportunity for social advancement, which was closed to them before the war, or they joined the militia in order to protect their community against 'bands'. Meanwhile, Poles often joined communist structures because they wanted to exercise power. An important element of these memories, undermining the hegemonic discourse, is the stories of former Polish anti-communist partisans who, despite their crimes, made careers in the state and party administration. As one interviewee said,

> this paradox was also that (...) some of these underground guys there later worked in the municipality. Here, there was one, we know whom he killed, when he killed, whom he robbed, and later he was a figure that this link between the underground and the authorities (...) those who were educated, after all, all of them were later in the municipality.

The presence of former partisans in the state administrations was another reason why the underground crimes were only talked about among those closest to them. There was also a perception that it was not in the interest of the authorities themselves to investigate the crimes of the underground, as evidenced, for example, by the concealment of information about the site of the crimes against the carters. The authorities avoided this issue – suggested the Belarusian interlocutors – because it could turn out that the underground's activities were to their advantage, as they fitted in with the communist plans for population exchange.

Some Belarusian interlocutors suggested that the partisans were murdering the local Belarusian population in some kind of agreement with the communists, and that the basis of their alignment was Polish ethnic nationalism and a desire for 'ethnic cleansing':

> I'm waiting until some historian finally dares to return to this topic of Bury's bloody raid and explains (...) how it's possible that (...) half a year after the war the village of Zaleszany is on fire (...) 4 km from this village there's a small town Kleszczele (...) there's a fire department there, everybody saw that Zaleszany was on fire, nobody came to help, the raid

lasted a week, 5 days (...) it's perhaps some kind of conspiracy theory, but there are many questions (...) in my opinion the communist authorities controlled this action, I tend to believe that 'Bury' was used for forced repatriation.

The interviewee recounts the bloody raid by Bury's unit in Podlasie, which we mentioned earlier. The anti-communist partisans burned down several Belarusian villages in early 1946 and murdered dozens of Belarusians. At the same time, the aforementioned population exchange was taking place. The interviewee speculates on the partisans' collaboration with the communists, which is an attempt to understand why the communists, who controlled state institutions, did not try to stop the partisans. Belarusian activists stressed that, against stereotypes, the communists were not enemies of Polishness; on the contrary, they wanted to build a nationally homogeneous Polish state implementing a de facto programme of Polish ethnic nationalists. From this perspective, the murder of Belorussian and Orthodox inhabitants in Podlasie by partisans was to the communists' advantage, because the intimidated population was more likely to leave for the Soviet Union, which brought the construction of an ethnically homogeneous Poland closer. It must be added, however, that not all interviewees shared this conviction that the partisans were collaborating with the communists, but there was often the conviction that after 1944 there was a kind of war of the partisans against the local Orthodox and Belorussian population. Thus, while the Polish Critics emphasised above all the general demoralisation and conditions under which the underground operated, the Belarusians emphasised to a much greater extent the views of the partisans themselves, especially those operating in Podlasie, as the cause of the various crimes against the Belarusian and Orthodox population. In their view, the underground aimed at ethnic and religious cleansing, which was in line with the traditional aim of Polish ethnic Catholic nationalists.

For the Apologists of the 'cursed soldiers', the views shared by our Belarusian interlocutors are remnants of communist propaganda. Meanwhile, from the point of view of the Belarusian informants, their negative attitude towards the underground, even if exaggerated, is the result of trauma, a genuine sense of injustice and a reaction to the glorification of criminals: 'I don't see any hero in Bury and I even think that just such figures did a lot of harm (...) through the prism of their notorious deeds, you look at those who did not act like that'. Belarusian interviewees placed the ethnic cleansing carried out by the underground in the broader framework and negative historical experience with the Polish state. In their view, they were the result of the fact that, from 1918 onwards, the nationalistic authorities of the II RP had pursued discriminatory actions towards minorities. This politics was rooted in long-lasting cultural structures dating back to the early modern period and the ideologies of the nobility's Christian antemurale and Sarmatism. These long-standing cultural imaginaries were based on the Polish sense of superiority over the Eastern Slavs and resorted to a xenophobic discourse to justify the colonisation of the 'wild' East. As one interviewee said, both the discrimination against the Belarusians in the past and the current memory politics have such deep roots: 'I have this conviction that it may also stem from some, so to speak, centuries-old Polish feeling, a feeling of superiority towards Eastern Slavs. Because the communism and the Soviet Union, Russia, that's where the evil came from'.

Interestingly, the interviewees saw the same contemptuous attitude towards Eastern Slavs in the anti-communist opposition under the banner of Solidarity in the 1980s, which they perceived as a nationalist and Catholic movement. In their view, Belarusians in the eyes of Podlasie Solidarity activists were part of the Soviet world, against which Solidarity rebelled. Therefore, many Belarusians perceived Solidarity in terms of the return of post-war anti-communism; they feared that the 'time of ethnic cleansing' would return again:

> I, as a child, did not know what was going to happen with this Solidarity, I only knew that it was something terrible. Solidarity and AK, but the AK had been gone, and Solidarity was here (…) all these extreme movements on the part of Poles, that they are a threat, are aimed at defending Polishness (…) and fighting against Belarusianness and Orthodoxy.

According to informants, the hegemonic memory politics echoes the narrative of the superiority of Catholic Poles over Orthodox Belarusians, who are attributed to belong to an inferior Eastern civilisation. This narrative accuses Belarusians of collaborating with Poland's enemies, especially with Russia in its various forms. At the same time, some informants note that the hegemonic politics often refers to a peculiar variation of the 'myth of the Judeo-Communism', where Jewish communists are replaced by Belarusian-Communists:

> this antagonism is particularly evident when you start any discussion about Bury, and those who are supporters of Bury, of the cursed soldiers, always say that we are the ones who represent this healthy nucleus (…) and you are all these husks, the descendants of the communists, the descendants of the criminals.

According to informants, this discourse of contempt functions in the mainstream memory discourse, as manifested by the open glorification of Bury, who has been included in the pantheon of national heroes. This negative depiction of Belarusians also resonates in the statements of key Polish officials such as President Andrzej Duda. On 7 June 2021, at the invitation of Belarusian activists, Duda came to Zaleszany and laid flowers at the cross commemorating the Belarusians murdered by the Bury unit, saying that this place is 'marked by suffering, marked by death, where people once died, where innocent women, children died'. The visit divided the Belarusian community. Some felt that it was a significant gesture. Others, however, felt that it was a conjunctural action designed to win over Belarusians but change nothing in the memory politics. According to the interviewees, the president upheld the official narrative by stating that 'the victims died' and not mentioning the name of the perpetrator of the crime. Some informants claimed that the president suggested that some of the victims deserved their fate because they collaborated with the communists:

> President was in Zaleszany for 3 hours listening to people (...) there was a voice from the floor, 'Mr President, this [Bury] glorification is too much', and he said something like this: 'Victims are victims, but I know that there were also collaborators' (...) He also joined this narrative, it is unbelievable, it is not even some kind of rage, genuinely people feel completely defenceless, they feel like second-class citizens.

Some Belarusian interlocutors interpreted the President's visit as being in keeping with the hegemonic memory politics, which is based on the denial that Polish troops murdered Belarusians. In their view, the President resorted to rhetoric that could be described as 'deserved punishment' – as we have seen such argumentation appearing in statements by Apologists.

Interviewees stressed that commemorating criminals like Bury not only evokes traumatic experiences and completely disregards the sensitivity of the victims' descendants but also shows that Poland is returning to its traditional politics of discrimination against Belarusians. This memory politics makes it clear to Belarusians that this is not their state and eradicates their historical experiences from the public sphere. One interviewee commented:

> this state does not want us at all, i.e. it wants us on the condition (...) that we will hide (...) people are afraid because they remember the old fear, this fear is revived from time to time, because you have probably already heard about the great return of fear during martial law, yes, about those crosses, about those stories, they were exactly the same clichés from that 1945–46 they came to life then (...) you cannot feel safe.

The hegemonic politics produces – to refer to our theoretical categories – a collective field of fear. This collective fear, in the eyes of the interviewee, is linked to the return of the post-war atmosphere of danger, which was again repeated in the 1980s. The interviewee speaks about the crosses as a reference to the stories circulating among the Belarusian population in the early 1980s – as mentioned earlier – that Solidarity was about to carry out ethnic cleansing. The crosses on the flats' doors were supposed to be used to identify who was 'ours' and who was 'other', which in turn is reminiscent of post-war times, when partisans decided on the basis of religion whether someone was 'our' Polish-Catholic or 'other'. To quote another rather symptomatic statement:

> People don't understand why this, why Bury, why Łupaszka, for what does Poland need this? Especially in such a place as Potoka, I was there a year ago, the locals built a chapel (...) it was burnt down twice by the first Łupaszka unit (...), there has been no investigation... there were children killed there too, only Orthodox, there is a plaque outside the chapel saying that some tragedy happened, very euphemistically, and the idea is to give inside a plaque in Belarusian (...) outside we give it so that no one breaks the window, but inside let's show the truth.

This statement illustrates the sense of injustice among the Belarusian interviewees, as well as their fear of speaking publicly about their experiences, as they are aware that this does not agree with the dominant message. In this context, a story can be quoted from one Belarusian employee of a media institution who prepared material presenting the post-war experiences of Belarusians for a wider audience. However, the material met with a negative reaction in the headquarters in Warsaw: 'What the fuck are you sending me? This is a series on national and ethnic minorities (...) you're supposed to show... how these minorities dance, sing (...) not the fuck how a Polish hero unit killed Belarusians'. This story illustrates a broader trend present in the public sphere, and prevalent in history education. Minorities are interesting insofar as they can be presented as a kind of addition to the dominant culture in which they fit. Minorities may cultivate some of their 'exotic' customs from time to time on festive occasions, but these must not come into conflict with the dominant culture (Jaskulowski et al., 2022).

This does not mean that there are no attempts to take various measures to increase the visibility of the Belarusian experience in the public space. These include attempts to politically mobilise the Belarusian population and create an electoral list and get their representation in parliament, but this is hampered by the dispersion of Belarusians and lack of organisational resources. There have also been attempts by Belarusians to obtain compensation for victims and descendants of partisan victims, but these have been unsuccessful (Czykwin, 2019). This reinforces the sense of injustice, as such compensation has been received by the descendants of 'Bury'. Belarusian activists also create memorials to the victims of the underground, publish books and compile archives, collecting the accounts of witnesses to the crimes and their descendants, but there are fewer and fewer of them due to age. In addition, older people are still afraid to talk about their experiences. The sense of injustice is also compounded by the fact that official institutions are not interested in these accounts. Nor do official institutions provide any support.

The interlocutors also indicated that the memory politics emboldens extreme nationalist circles to openly proclaim slogans of hatred, as demonstrated by the marches in honour of Bury organised by ethnic-authoritarian nationalists (referring to the pre-war Polish fascist organisations – the aforementioned ONR and All-Polish Youth (MW)) in Hajnówka, a municipality largely inhabited by Belarusians. Belarusian interlocutors stressed that they found it difficult to understand the lack of reaction from the Polish state. As they stressed, despite the fact that the marches feature slogans calling for violence, e.g. 'death to the enemies of the motherland', as well as Nazi and racist symbols banned by law in Poland, the prosecutor's office has repeatedly discontinued the investigation. As one Belarusian activist said,

> we compare this march with the Nazi march in Auschwitz (...) I am accused, but after all, only 79 people died (...) but if, as it were, the aim was intimidation, not death and not execution, this was a sufficient number, because listen, imagine between 44 and 47 thirty-something thousand people left... left these villages forever, and those who stayed were traumatised for the rest of their lives (...) unfortunately this atmosphere for the last few years, which has been in Poland, only fuels this spiral.

Similar links also appear in public statements by Belarusian activists and show the role of the Jewish experience as a reference point for framing the situation in which the Belarusian minority finds itself. Such statements, as in the case of the right wing, can be interpreted as an instrumentalisation of the Holocaust. However, while the right wing uses the Holocaust to legitimise its exclusionary hegemonic memory project, the interviewee invokes this symbolism to highlight the trauma experienced by members of a subordinated group confronted with marches in honour of the perpetrators of ethnic cleansing.

While the hegemonic politics instrumentalises the Holocaust to legitimise its exclusionary project based on the logic of 'competitive memory', Belarusian activists use the symbol of Auschwitz to stress the trauma experienced by members of a marginalised minority group. Here, the memory of the Holocaust becomes a discursive vehicle for the Belarusian experience of persecution and suffering, which does not attempt to compete for uniqueness with Jewish memory but serves to universalise the experience of a marginalised group with low status and limited resources. Under conditions of asymmetrical power relations, less influential Belarusian 'memory makers' mobilise the rhetoric of the Holocaust to challenge the hegemonic politics of memory and strengthen the legitimacy of their narratives about the past and increase the visibility and significance of their traumatic historical experiences in the public space. In this sense, this critique of hegemonic memory politics by Belarusian scholars can be seen as a form of 'multidirectional memory' (Rothberg, 2009), in which the Holocaust is not the object of appropriation

Heroes? Partisans? Bandits? The 'Cursed Soldiers' from Below 95

and contestation but the context of a struggle for the rights of an underprivileged minority with its own traumatic experiences.

In this context, it is important to mention that some critics had concerns that the right-wing memory politics, by placing the 'cursed soldiers' at its centre, performs if not directly then indirectly the function of normalising Nazism and may legitimise violence in relations with minorities. Interviewees were afraid that the memory politics marginalises the traditions of the struggle against the German occupation and suggests that communism was a greater threat than Nazism, which in a way legitimises far-right ideologies. To some of the interviewees, the very symbolism and aesthetics of the 'cursed soldiers' resembled Nazism. They underlined that the 'cursed soldiers' are often symbolically depicted as a wolf, which they associated with the Nazi Werwolf formations. They also argued that the commemoration takes the form of various sporting competitions, which to them reminds them of the cult of physical strength characteristic of fascism. The colour scheme of the marches and patriotic clothing evokes similar associations: 'it's such a black styling I just somehow associate it with Hitler, maybe it's not like that, or maybe that's how the symbolism is supposed to be associated'. And, according to the interviewee, the fashion for 'patriotic' clothing or music with the theme of 'the cursed soldiers' demonstrates that these militaristic and fascist aesthetics are becoming increasingly popular in Polish society, becoming a carrier of dangerous extreme nationalist ideas.

Both Polish and Belarusian critics thus assessed the underground as a whole very negatively, which was also reflected in the fact that instead of the well-connoted word 'soldier' they used pejorative terms: 'bandits', 'marauders', 'fur-coaters' (because partisans looted clothes). Some, however, preferred the neutral term 'partisans' or 'forester men' because they wanted to avoid the emotional labelling that is a reversal of what the hegemonic memory politics does: 'I try to use neutral terms (...) not to do what our historical politics does'. Despite their negative attitude towards the memory politics and the underground in general, not all Critics subscribed fully to the oppositional reading. Rather, some took a negotiated position, i.e. they disagreed with commemorating the PPP as a whole and under the name of 'cursed soldiers' or 'indomitable soldiers', believing that these were highly ideologised symbols. However, some Critics felt that some partisans deserved the status of national heroes: 'then there is never such a feeling that about all the cursed soldiers were criminals, in general nobody would dare to say something like that'.

Critics therefore allowed for selective commemoration of partisans, although they differed when it came to selection criteria. Two positions can be distinguished. Some Critics indicated that the need to commemorate partisans is understandable, but one cannot commemorate 'someone who committed a crime'. It is not so much the underground as a whole that should be commemorated but the actual individual figures with the exception of those who murdered people. At the same time, those Critics assumed that there were relatively few such partisans who committed crimes. The second position was dominant and characterised by greater scepticism. More sceptical Critics argued that the underground as a whole had a tendency towards banditry and committing various crimes. It is only possible to commemorate, by way of exception, some partisans, but such figures worth commemorating were rather few in number. As one interviewee said, 'it is worth commemorating individuals like Pilecki'. Critics also objected to elevating the 'cursed soldiers' to the status of a key memorial symbol and postulated: 'to see this problem through the lens of the common people (…) because innocent people died at the hands of those people who are now called cursed soldiers'.

Outsiders

The last category is a small group of Outsiders, who subversively accepted the notion of 'cursed soldiers' but gave it a meaning that undermined the hegemonic memory politics. Three types of argumentation can be distinguished here. The first group of interviewees emphasised their distance from the hegemonic politics by adopting an ironic strategy. This group included interlocutors characterised by higher education and a relatively high social position. The interviewees did not have traumatic family memories related to the underground either, so it was easy for them to maintain an emotional distance. Thus, they joked that 'cursed soldiers' was a very accurate term, but in reference to the soldiers of the Polish army fighting alongside the Soviet army against the Third Reich, the People's Army, i.e. the communist partisans, or the Polish volunteers fighting during the Spanish Civil War in the 1930s on the side of the Republic. On a more serious note, they added that the ruling right reproduces the patterns of the forgetting policy of authoritarian regimes by creating its own system of exclusion. This system is based on a simple moralistic binary opposition: 'us' versus 'them', 'good' versus 'evil', Poles versus communists. Any attempt to argue that historical reality was more complex is treated by the right wing as an undermining of the natural God-given moral order that threatens some sort of axiological catastrophe. And yet, argued the interviewees, the post-war reality was more complex and many former AK partisans joined the Polish army or the militia and fought with their former colleagues. A democratic state should not turn history into a moralistic fairy tale but take into account the sensitivities and experiences of different groups in its remembrance policy,

> to commemorate both of them there, that is to say that they were simply the de facto victims of some kind of fratricidal struggle, or even without any affiliation as to who was a hero, who was not, that they simply died a tragic death there.

The ironic strategy was also referred to by some interviewees defining themselves in terms of Silesian national identity – the second type of argumentation. Here, it should be noted that according to the census, the Silesians are the largest national minority in Poland, yet the Polish state does not recognise the Silesian nationality, and the right wing frames Silesian activists as dangerous extremists (Kamusella, 2012). Obviously, it is difficult to place all Silesians in this pattern, as some with conservative views identified with the post-war partisans to the extent that they fought the communists. However, at the same time, these interviewees disassociated themselves from the hegemonic memory politics of the 'cursed soldiers' because it glorified partisans who carried out purges of national minorities instead of fighting the communists. As one interviewee said, 'Bury and Ogień are figures that are downright disgraceful in relation to those who fought the communists (…) this is an example of the degeneration of the memory politics'.

Most of our Silesian interlocutors took the position of a kind of external observer in relation to the narrative of the 'cursed soldiers', which clearly distinguishes them from Belarusian Critics. In contrast to Belarusian Critics, stories about partisans did not circulate in the communicative memory of Silesian interlocutors. This history is not an identity reference point for them because, in their view, it does not belong to the Silesian past and has not become element of Silesian collective memory. As one interviewee briefly explained, '"Bury", "Inka" (…) is not a piece of our history'. The lack of traumatic experiences and the perception of the history of the underground as something external translated into an ironic attitude on the part of some interviewees towards the memory politics: 'a joke was circulating that our cursed soldiers are Werwolf'. The interlocutors were reacting to the hegemonic symbolic politics that depicts people declaring Silesian nationality as a German 'covert option'. He ridiculed anti-Silesian stereotypes by referring to the caricatured image of the Silesian, who allegedly identifies with the Third Reich and celebrates the Nazi partisans. Behind the irony was the notion that the hegemonic memory politics ignores completely local experiences that do not fit into the 'Warsaw-centric' conception of history. One such local experience is the forced service of Silesians in the Wehrmacht, which the hegemonic politics of memory presents as 'treason' (Jaskulowski & Majewski, 2020).

The interviewees look at the symbolism of the 'cursed soldiers' from a distance without feeling that it relates to their history and experiences, but at the same time they highlight two negative consequences of this memory politics for the Silesian national minority. First, the hegemonic memory politics is another tool for reinforcing the dominant Polish-centric vision of the past. From their point of view, PiS further consolidates the narrative already prevailing in, for example, historical education, which is focused on the history of a narrowly defined Polish nation. This conception is ethnic and, as they put it, 'Warsaw-centric'. It has no place for the narratives and experiences of other ethnic and national groups that contribute to Polish society: 'it is clearly mono-ethnic, that is, the memory of the cursed soldiers is the memory of chauvinists and nationalists who fought quite openly against national minorities'.

Second, according to the interviewees, the right-wing memory politics not only falsifies the past but also portrays minority groups in an unequivocally negative light, dividing Polish society into 'real Poles' and their enemies, who are attributed with non-Polish nationality (as if this were a bad thing) and/or with actions in favour of foreign interests. As one interviewee explains,

> the authorities, through such a myth (...) of an indomitable Pole, show that a part of the citizens can call themselves Poles, because these are the ones who carry the legacy of the indomitable soldiers, while all the rest are harlots and servants of Germany, Russia, Jews (...) we show what Poland really is (...) where Poland was (...) that it was in the forest (...) that we are moving this Poland from the forest here to these institutions, to Nowogrodzka Street [the offices of PiS].

Thus, the interviewees look at the history of the 'cursed soldiers' with detachment and declare that the disputes about the underground are 'Polish disputes' that are external to their experiences. At the same time, however, this politics affects them due to its antagonistic nature.

At the same time, paradoxically, although interviewees criticise this hegemonic memory politics for appealing to a sense of pride and superiority, some interviewees themselves appeal to a kind of superiority. The interviewees look at members of the Polish national community with a certain irony, if not derision. In their view, the memory politics of 'cursed soldiers' is yet another example of the Polish authoritarian nationalism, anti-Semitism, martyrdom complex and the mechanism of falsification of the past built into the dominant Polish collective memory:

> Students are told that we regained our independence, then we painstakingly built our statehood, which was basically cool (...), and they are not taught that we were practically the poorest country in Europe with mega-social inequalities, but it was cool, because if it had gone on like that, we would have had colonies (...) and we would have basically competed with the biggest economies and countries in the world. But then came Hitler, then came the communists and (...) came another betrayal and again, you know, Poland, which after all should have its rightful place in the world, can't have that place, and we still have to sit in this forest like those cursed soldiers (...), by this campfire we can make plans on how to regain that greatness again and sing 'Whisky my wife'.

This ironic attitude reveals that the 'cursed soldiers' symbolism performs certain identity functions for Silesians. These functions are incompatible with the intentions of the creators of this politics, since the interviewees define their Silesianness in opposition to Polishness, perceiving the latter as something somehow inferior. Our interviewees referred to a kind of 'soft' xenophobic discourse, which consists in constructing a negative stereotype of the 'Other', the typical Pole, and in contrasting this stereotype with their own community:

> In Silesia it looks different (...) the most important thing is what happens in the immediate environment (...) let's say, in inverted commas of course: the street, the city, the region and only then Poland. (...) and these patriotic groups (...) we will go to shoot and die for the homeland (...) just as in Russia you get love for mother Russia, here you get love for mother Poland, and this is supposed to be a substitute for a good quality of life there.

The attitude to the hegemonic memory politics thus allowed our Silesian interlocutors to distinguish themselves from the Polish majority, to assert their Silesian otherness or their Silesian nationalism as something better, more rational, open, and democratic than the aggressive, exclusionary and militarised Polish nationalism. They define their own Silesian nationalism in terms of a modern 'Western European', open and civic nationalism, whereas they essentialised and 'orientalised' Polish nationalism as a manifestation of an 'Eastern' and ethnic nationalism based on a logic of exclusion:

> I think it shows some complexes (...) that Poles have a problem (...) that one can be a normal person without beating another in the head with a baton (...) This is not just a Polish problem, we have seen it in the Balkans, we see it in Ukraine, it is happening in Russia. I think that it concerns societies that are not fully able to cope with their own history, because they believe that they are unique.

This argumentation resembles a 'strategy of discursive substitution', which is a form of civic exclusion using the logic of ethnic exclusion (Fozdar & Low, 2015). Some Silesians, while defining their own nationalism as open, at the same time tended to construct Polishness in essentialist terms as irrational and incompatible with democratic institutions.

The interviewees also see in these terms the manifestation of Polish and Silesian nationalisms in everyday life (Billig, 1995; Edensor, 2002). This can be seen in the perceived pop culturalisation and commodification of national identity in the form of 'patriotic clothing'. According to the Silesian interviewees, Polish patriotic clothing reproduces an authoritarian discourse of hostility towards other nations, evokes 'grand' mythologised stories of Poland's power, and calls for political mobilisation. The message of Silesian clothing, however, in the eyes of the interviewees, is not political but rather focuses on the everyday, the local, and the homelike and is meant to promote a Silesian identity that is open to others. As the interviewee explained,

> there are no political elements here, there are no mythological elements (...). it is more everyday (...) we live in a region where another language is used besides Polish and simply this language is applied to some products, and these products are not to fight, I mean they have not been created to build some myths, to build tools to fight anything (...) they are simply funny slogans.

According to the Silesian interviewees, Silesian clothing has a completely different emotional charge and has a different purpose:

> Until pop culture gadgets associated with Silesia appeared, it was harder to convince young people that this Silesian identity was cool (...). It was something older people talked about (...) now I can have a cool sweatshirt, I can have a cool bag (...). And it also helps a lot (...) if I see a Coca Cola advert in Silesian, that means it's something cool (...) But this Polish narrative is so exclusionary of the others and only we who support the cursed soldiers are the good patriots, and all the rest are bad (...) a narrative built on such hostility, on violence, there is always blood somewhere, wolves. This Silesian pop culture is always so positive (...) it doesn't try to build this image on any war, but only on the Silesian language or some other elements of culture, which are neutral, and here, all the time, this element of violence, these black, white and red colours, they build such aggression, hostility, so completely different emotions.

The interlocutors look at hegemony memory politics with a certain anxiety and concern about its negative consequences for the position of national minorities, but at the same time with a certain ironic distance and a sense of superiority. The interviewees draw a kind of 'lesson' from this observation not to build the collective memory of Silesians on a deformed image of the past, martyrdom and the myth of sacrifice. They draw a vision of building a Silesian collective memory mainly on communicative memory, personal memories, local memories, and not on cultural memory, 'grand' canonical narratives fixed in textbooks or in monumental statues:

> I don't know if, because of the mythologisation of this notion, would we here, as Silesians, want our [Silesians who were in the Wehrmacht] to be like the cursed soldiers? These are rather intimate home stories, that is, we do not build pathos around these people here, (...) we are aware (...) that every second grandparent was simply in the Wehrmacht and could have suppressed the Warsaw Uprising (...) could have shot innocent

Heroes? Partisans? Bandits? The 'Cursed Soldiers' from Below 101

people and I think that as a group we are (…) far from mythologising. (…) I don't think that if, for example, Silesia had autonomy, in 20 years' time we would be taught in textbooks that they are heroes (…) they are people thrust into the tragic vortex of history.

Other Silesian interlocutors, as we have already noted, were ironic about the right-wing politics and said that it was their ancestors who had served in the Wehrmacht who should today be referred to as the real 'cursed soldiers'. They indicated that the official memory politics is based on forgetting this fact or even stigmatising them as 'traitors', while their ancestors were not in the German army of their own free will but were forcibly conscripted, and many of them later suffered repression from the Polish and Soviet communist authorities for this:

I can answer jokingly that in Upper Silesia there are voices claiming that it is our relatives, the German soldiers, who deserve the name of cursed soldiers, because they are still cursed. And you can still hear the accusation that someone had a grandfather in the wrong army.

In this way, the interviewees capture, in a sense, the notion of 'cursedness', which originally conveyed an ideology in line with the interests of the ruling right, in order to use it in a subversive form to combat the dominant order and give it a meaning contrary to the cultural hegemony stabilising that order (Storey, 2021). This procedure is a form of immanent critique, conducted, as it were, from within the discourse to which it refers, and involves the non-normative use of the language of the dominant group for its own purposes.

However, Silesian interviewees use the concept of 'cursed' for their own purposes, not only in the context of constructing a story about Silesians serving in the Wehrmacht. They often also refer to the victims of Polish Soviet repression in 1945 as 'cursed'. In early 1945, after the Red Army entered Upper Silesia, the persecution of the indigenous population began. The repressions included looting, mass rape and murder, and deportation deep into the Soviet Union mainly for forced labour, especially in the mines. These actions, which resulted in the deaths of tens of thousands of people, were largely a form of revenge against the Germans. The complex national situation in Upper Silesia meant that the victims of the camps located in Silesia were mainly autochthones (Silesians), who were mistaken for Germans (Kulczycki, 2016). Under communist rule, it was forbidden to speak or write about the Upper Silesian Tragedy, and it was only after 1989 that people began to record the memories of the living, carry out research, collect documents, write about this tragic period for the people of Upper Silesia and commemorate the victims (Woźniczka, 2010). Despite this, however, the memory/knowledge of the Upper Silesian Tragedy did not become an element of Polish public discourse and Polish collective memory, functioning, as an important 'figure of memory', mainly among Silesians:

> Well, and it's such a painful issue, about which I didn't learn from school that these concentration camps were still in operation. It wasn't until I was 17 that I went to a conference on the Upper Silesian Tragedy, and asked about the camp where I knew my great-grandfather and great-grandmother had been (...) IPN did not even know that this camp existed (...) well, it is difficult to use this word, but 'cursed' simply on the basis that we are not allowed to talk about it, because then there is immediately a narration that, well, because you were Germans, so you deserved it. (...) So the message we still get is: you have to know your place in the line.

For these Silesian interviewees, it is not so much the history of the post-war anti-communist partisans that deserves to be called 'the cursed' but the past of the minority groups that make up Polish society, which has never, including before PiS took power in 2015, been put on a par with the dominant Polish memory discourse:

> Speaking of this similarity of history between Silesia and the cursed soldiers (...) A few years ago there was a historical walk in Bieruń and it was mainly through the cemetery. And they stopped, and I heard it from the parents that they stopped at the grave of the former headmaster of the school, there was praising how wonderful he was, and then the grandmother came home crying and it turned out that he had taught her when she was about seven years old and he said that we will pave the roads here with those German skulls of yours, so in fact this is such an unprocessed lesson and there is no room for this other narrative. There is only this uncritical narrative.

The third type of argumentation is taking the perspective of civilians, which also appeared in other argumentative strategies. The interviewee's statement below illustrates this perspective:

> they were mocked doubly, by the authorities of the time and (...) by the people ... especially from the countryside. The people suffered because of their actions (...) the partisans (...) also caused a lot of damage (...) that was never spoken of (...) they sat in these forests and tried to do something there (...) they managed to set up an ambush, killed one German soldier, and the whole village either went up in smoke or ended up in Auschwitz (...) people didn't like this kind of activity, because if you survived and managed to keep some cows, they'd come to you at night and give you something to eat, because we have nothing to eat, and we're fighting for your freedom (...) there was freedom after all, because Hitler didn't exist

Heroes? Partisans? Bandits? The 'Cursed Soldiers' from Below

(…) everyone wants to live! And not to play forever in some kind of herding in the woods.

This is an interesting statement – the interviewee treats the Second World War partisans fighting against the Germans and post-war partisans as one category. He breaks a national taboo by saying that the partisans fighting the Germans did not enjoy the support of the local population because they brought repression on the local population. The post-war partisans are described by the interviewee in disparaging terms as 'scouting'. Some interviewees in this context added that the partisans were even 'cursed' by the Church, which disassociated itself from them after the war in recognition of the need to rebuild the country. Contrary to the official discourse of the two occupations, the interviewee quoted believes that the end of the Second World War meant freedom, i.e. the end of the occupation personified by Hitler. The end of the occupation offered hope for stability and a normal life, which the partisans made difficult or impossible. At the same time, the interviewee notes that the negative effects of the partisans are not discussed in public at all. This belief in the one-sidedness of the public debate also appears, as we have seen, in the statements of the Critics, who stressed that the official memory politics ignores the perspective of the civilian population in general, and especially the point of view of the victims of the underground.

References

Banks, M. (2001). *Visual methods in social research*. London: Sage.
Billig, M. (1995). *Banal nationalism*. London: Sage.
Bourdieu, P. (1984). *Distinction: A social critique of the judgement of taste*. Cambridge, MA: Harvard University Press
Bourdieu, P. P. (1993). *Sociology in question*. London: Sage.
CBOS. (2017). *Polskie podziemie antykomunistyczne w pamięci zbiorowej [Polish anti-communist underground in the collective memory]*. Warsaw: CBOS.
Cohen, A. P. (1985). *The symbolic construction of community*. New York: Tavistock.
Czykwin, E. (2000). *Białoruska mniejszość narodowa jako grupa sygmatyzowana [Belarusian national minority as a sigmatised group]*. Białystok: Trans Humana.
Czykwin, E. (Ed.) (2019). *Żołnierze wyklęci. Białostocczyzna 1945–1947 [Cursed soldiers. Białystok region 1945–1947]*. Białystok: Fundacja im. Ks. Konstantego Ostrogskiego.
Dobrosielski, P. (2017). *Spory o Grossa [Disputes over Gross]*. Warsaw: IBL.
Edensor, T. (2002). *National identity, popular culture and everyday life*. Oxford: Berg.
Foucault, M. (1977). *Language, counter-memory, practice: Selected essays and interviews*. Ithaca, NY: Cornell University Press.
Fozdar, F., & Low, M. (2015). 'They have to abide by our laws … and stuff': Ethnonationalism masquerading as civic nationalism. *Nations and Nationalism, 21*(3), 524–543.
Geertz, C. (1988). *Work and lives. The anthropologist as author*. Stanford: Stanford University Press.

Hall, S. (1980). Encoding/decoding. In S. Hall, D. Hobson, A. Lowe, & P. Willis (Eds.), *Culture, media, language* (pp. 128–138). London: Hutchinson.

Jaskulowski, K. (2019). *The everyday of politic of the migration crisis in Poland.* Cham: Palgrave.

Jaskulowski, K., & Kilias, J. (2016). Polityka nacjonalistycznej rewolucji. Studio Opinii. Retrieved from http://studioopinii.pl/archiwa/164532

Jaskulowski, K., & Majewski, P. (2020). Politics of memory in Upper Silesian schools: Between Polish homogeneous nationalism and its Silesian discontents. *Memory Studies, 13*(1), 60–73.

Jaskulowski, K., Majewski, P., & Surmiak, A. (2022). *Teaching history, celebrating nationalism: School history education in Poland.* London and New York: Routledge.

Kamusella, T. (2009). *The politics of language and nationalism in modern Central Europe.* London: Palgrave.

Kamusella, T. (2012). Poland and the Silesians: Minority rights à la carte? *Journal of Ethnopolitics and Minority Issues in Europe, 11*(2), 42–74.

Kilias, J. (2004). *Wspólnota abstrakcyjna [Abstract community].* Warsaw: IFiS PAN.

Kulczycki, J. (2016) *Belonging to the nation: Inclusion and exclusion in the Polish–German Borderlands, 1939–1951.* Cambridge, MA: Harvard University Press.

Morley, D. (2006). Unanswered questions in audience research. *The Communication Review, 9*(2), 101–121.

Rothberg, M. (2009). *Multidirectional memory: Remembering the holocaust in the age of decolonization.* Stanford: Stanford University Press.

Schrøder, K. Ch. (2000). Making sense of audience discourses: Towards a multidimensional model of mass media reception. *European Journal of Cultural Studies, 3*(2) 233–258.

Storey, J. (2021). *Cultural theory and popular culture: An introduction.* London: Routledge.

Strauss, A., & Corbin, J. M. (1998). *Basics of qualitative research.* Thousand Oaks, CA: Sage.

Woźniczka, Z. (2010). *Represje Na Górnym Śląsku Po 1945 Roku [Repression in Upper Silesia after 1945].* Katowice: Śląsk.

Zychowicz, P. (2018). *Skazy na pancerzach [Flaws on armour].* Warsaw: Rebis.

6 Between Radicalisation and Contestation

The book analyses the collective memory of the post-war underground in Poland understood as a dynamic process of production and reception taking place under conditions of hegemonic structures of memory. This hegemonic context is determined by the right-wing memory politics, which transformed the underground into an ideological and emotionally charged symbol of the 'cursed soldiers'. PiS has elevated the figure of the 'cursed soldiers' to the status of a key memorial symbol that condenses a whole range of ideological meanings and builds an emotional collective field around the pride, bravery, suffering, and exceptionality of the Polish nation. The symbol is the simple and tangible representation of a right-wing memory project that aims to remodel Polish collective memory according to right-wing notions of the Polish nation as a patriarchal Catholic and conservative community defined in terms of a 'thick' culture. This antagonistic memory regime underpins the right-wing symbolic politics of moral renewal of the Polish nation allegedly being in deep cultural crisis. This process of hegemony-building is still in progress, as our analyses of the reception of the symbolism of the 'cursed soldiers' demonstrates.

We analysed the intensification of memory politics of the 'cursed soldiers' in the context of three processes: institutionalisation, symbolic thickening, and popularisation. PiS institutionalised the commemoration by consolidating and strengthening the presence of 'cursed soldiers' in the calendar of official days, cultural policy, and education. In the process of symbolic thickening, PiS assigned to the symbol a whole series of meanings and emotions in line with its ideology. It has inscribed the 'cursed soldiers' in the tradition of national liberation struggles as another national uprising against communism. The party frames communism in line with the logic of the discourse of the two totalitarianisms as equivalent to Nazism. The glorification of the post-war partisans here goes hand in hand with a discourse of martyrdom and rivalry of suffering that constructs Poland as a victim of two equally criminal totalitarianisms. In this context, the 'cursed soldiers' symbolise national boundaries, between 'us' the true Poles and the rest, and personify the fate of the Polish nation persecuted by the communists. At the same time, communism

DOI: 10.4324/9781003368847-6
This chapter has been made available under a CC-BY-NC-ND 4.0 license.

is regarded as external to Polish history and projected onto various 'others'. The popularisation of the symbolism of the 'cursed soldiers' includes the promotion of patriotic rap by various institutions. Under the guise of rebellion against the establishment, patriotic rappers reproduce a hegemonic memorial project using pop-cultural aesthetics. However, PiS does not have total control over the rappers, who radicalise the hegemonic by using more blunt and violent language, a more open glorification of violence and a more pronounced nostalgia for the patriarchal world of male brotherhood and heroism, which opens up a space for further radicalisation of the discourse of the 'cursed soldiers'.

Our analysis demonstrates that the antagonistic memorial project of PiS is far from being accepted, and that the symbolism of the 'cursed soldiers' is variously interpreted, provokes resistance and arouses conflicting emotions. The main dispute does not coincide with how PiS frames the conflict. The party defines the conflict in dichotomous terms as a dispute between those who support commemoration of the 'cursed soldiers' and those who reject this memory. It sees the acceptance of the whole mythical-symbolic complex associated with the 'cursed soldiers', feeling pride in them as national heroes as a condition of being Polish. According to this 'thick' cultural-emotional definition of Polishness, it excludes from the public space all those who disagree with this politics as non-Poles. In PiS's view, the public space must be monopolised by the symbols and memories of the titular nation defined narrowly in terms of a patriarchal Catholic ethnocultural community. This is met with resistance. What is objectionable is the commemoration of the underground en bloc under the ideologically charged term 'cursed soldiers' or 'indomitable soldiers', the ignoring of the 'dark' sides of the underground and the crimes against the civilian population, especially against national minorities. The memory politics arouses particularly vivid and strong emotions among Belarusians. It glorifies partisans whom the state institutions themselves have recognised as perpetrators of genocide. It comes into conflict with the Belarusian communicative memory, which stores traumatic memories of violence and killing. Belarusians have a sense of injustice and feel that they are denied public acknowledgement of their emotions, which do not fit into the collective field of pride, so they are repressed. This is accompanied by the fear that the Polish state is returning to its traditional politics of discrimination against Belarusians. Added to this is the sense of powerlessness associated with the lack of influence over the memory politics. The state ignores their efforts to obtain compensation for the victims, it does not support the gathering of testimonies of the few witnesses of the crimes who are still alive, and state institutions are not interested in the testimonies that have already been collected. Belarusians find it difficult to organise themselves due to limited resources and dispersion, although they engage in memorial activism and for example try to attract media attention. In this context, some activists resort to the symbolism of the Holocaust, which becomes a discursive vehicle for

Between Radicalisation and Contestation 107

the Belarusian experience of persecution and suffering that does not try to compete for uniqueness with Jewish memory but serves to universalise the experience of a marginalised group with low status, and limited power and resources.

Belarusians know that they cannot eradicate the dominant memory, but they hope that their voice and experiences can be more visible in the public space, thus expanding memoryscapes. Taking their experiences into account creates an opportunity for a more agonistic memory regime. However, institutional support and greater openness to oral accounts are needed. The state should also help collect the accounts of Polish victims of the underground – not to reactivate the myth of Polish suffering or to marginalise the experiences of minorities, but to go beyond simple national-centric schemes. The post-war struggle was not a conflict between Poles and minorities. It was a conflict of Polish authoritarian-ethnic nationalists with minorities and all those who deviated from their ideal of the anti-communist Pole-Catholic.

Index

agonistic memory politics 2, 6, 7, 29, 105, 107
anti-communism 7, 8, 26, 27, 28, 29, 30, 31, 33, 36, 37, 39, 40, 42, 43, 47, 59, 77, 80, 84, 88, 89, 90, 91, 102, 103
anti-Semitism 21, 25, 38, 42–50, 62, 68, 98
Auschwitz 19, 47, 48, 61, 62, 63, 94, 102
authoritarian nationalism 1, 6, 41, 45, 98

Belarusians 7, 64, 77, 78, 82, 87, 88, 89, 90, 91, 92, 93, 94, 106, 107

Catholic Church 12, 31, 36, 37, 40, 75
Catholicism 1, 12, 13, 21, 30, 40, 41, 59, 61, 81
civic nationalism 10, 99, 103
Civic Platform (Platforma Obywatelska, PO) 33, 36, 37, 77
civil war 24, 25, 26, 60, 76
Class 24, 25, 71
collective emotional field 5, 16, 17, 24, 92
collective memory, definition 14
cultural racism 13

The Democratic Left Alliance (Sojusz Lewicy Demokratycznej, SLD) 35, 36, 77.
displaced desire 55
Dmowski, R. 12, 17, 19, 39, 63
Dostoevsky, F. 42
Durkheim, E. 40, 61

'Easternness' 45
Eastern Slavs 91
Elzenberg, H. 28
ethnic cleansing 2, 4, 6, 10, 22, 52, 89, 90, 91, 92, 94

ethnic nationalism 10, 18, 89, 99
Europe 7, 10, 13, 20, 29, 30, 31, 41, 48, 49, 60, 64, 66, 98, 104

gender 5, 18, 38, 41, 54, 56, 62, 64, 65, 66
genocide 22, 42, 62, 63, 106
Germany 13, 22, 24, 44, 45, 98

Hajnówka 38, 94
hegemonic masculinity 54
hegemony 1–2, 14–17
Herbert, Z. 28
Hitler, A. 20, 65, 95, 98, 102, 103
holocaust 23, 42, 43, 45, 47, 48, 53, 60, 61, 63, 66, 94, 104, 106
Home Army (Armia Krajowa, AK) 20, 21, 22, 24, 25, 26, 47, 51, 56, 57, 75, 79, 83, 89, 91, 96

incorporation 4, 33, 50–51, 58
indomitable soldiers 60, 62, 64, 80, 81, 82, 83, 95, 98, 106
Institute of National Remembrance (Instytut Pamięci Narodowej, IPN) 3, 7, 11, 22, 23, 27, 30, 33–35, 36, 38, 39, 40, 43, 44, 45, 48, 51, 58, 60, 61, 62, 64, 65, 83, 89, 102

January Uprising 40
Jews 12, 21, 22, 26, 27, 33, 34, 38, 39, 43–50, 54, 60, 61, 76, 77, 78, 83, 98

Kaczyński, L. 35, 36, 63
Karski, J. 47
key memory symbol 1, 5, 15, 33, 42, 96, 105
Kościuszko Uprising 40
Kurtyka, J. 33, 34, 60, 64

Index

Law and Justice Party (Prawo i
  Sprawiedliwość, PiS) 1, 2, 3, 5, 6,
  11–17, 22, 32, 33, 35, 36, 38, 39, 40,
  42, 43, 44, 46, 50, 51, 52, 53, 60, 67,
  70, 72, 75, 81, 82, 83, 85, 97, 98,
  102, 105, 106

Maquis 20, 29
melancholy 55
memorial activism 32, 106
Memorial March of Cursed Soldiers 38
militaristic nationalism 24
Młyński, A. 86
Moczar, M., 24–27, 30
Museum of Cursed Soldiers and Political
  Prisoners of the Polish People's
  Republic in Warsaw 2, 39
Museum of Cursed Soldiers in Ostrołęka
  2, 39
Myth of the Judeo-Communism 21, 38,
  45, 48, 61, 76, 78, 79

Nazism 20, 26, 27, 29, 36, 38, 43, 44,
  45, 46, 47, 48, 53, 55, 57, 68, 94, 95,
  97, 105
National Armed Forces (Narodowe Siły
  Zbrojne, NSZ 20, 22, 24, 26, 35, 38,
  39, 62, 63
National Armed Forces – Polish
  Organisation (Narodowa Siły
  Zbrojne – Organizacja Polska,
  NSZ – OP) 22
National Day of Remembrance of Cursed
  Soldiers 36
National Democracy (Narodowa
  Demokracja) 11, 12
nationalism, definition 9–10
National Military Union (Narodowe
  Zjednoczenie Wojskowe,
  NZW) 22
National Radical Camp 26
November Uprising 40

Orientalism 49
Orthodox 87, 88, 90, 91, 93

Pantheon of Cursed soldiers 37
Piasecki, B. 26, 30, 31
Pilecki, W. 38, 39, 44, 46, 47, 48, 60, 61,
  62, 68, 83, 96
Podlasie 2, 4, 6, 22, 87, 88, 90, 91

Polishness 1, 12, 13, 21, 25, 41, 44, 45,
  49, 52, 53, 55, 58, 59, 63, 75, 79, 83,
  90, 91, 99, 106
Polish People's Party (Polskie
  Stronnictwo Ludowe, PSL) 21, 33,
  37, 84
'Polocaust' 46, 53, 64
popular culture 50

Rajs 'Bury' R. 4, 7, 22, 23, 38, 42, 61,
  64, 65, 78, 79, 85, 90, 91, 92, 93,
  94, 97
Red Army 21, 101
Republican League (LR) 27–28
Resistance Movement without War
  and Diversion 'Freedom and
  Independence' (Ruch Oporu bez
  Wojny i Dywersji 'Wolność i
  Niezawisłość', WiN) 21, 22, 33, 35, 38
Russia 12, 13, 36, 41, 45, 91, 98, 99
Russians 12, 41, 45, 76

Sarmatism 90
Schmitt, C. 11, 19
Scholl, S. 47
Siedzikówna 'Inka' D. 25, 40, 41, 42, 44,
  46, 47, 56, 60, 62, 68, 96, 97
Silesian national identity 96
Ślaski, Jerzy 3, 8, 26, 27, 31
Smolensk 13, 36
Solidarity 29, 31, 34, 77, 91, 92
Soviet Union 12, 20, 21, 25, 26, 45, 78,
  84, 87, 90, 91, 101
Spanish Civil War 96
Świetokrzyska Brigade 22
Szendzielarz 'Łupaszka', Z. 35

Third Republic (III RP) 27, 28, 31, 33,
  51, 75, 84
totalitarianism 6, 44, 45, 46, 47, 105
Treblinka camp 44, 62
Tygodnik Przegląd 32

Ukrainians 45

Wajda, A. 24
Warsaw Uprising 20, 21, 29, 62, 81, 100
We Remember Foundation 27, 35
Werwolf 95, 97

Zaleszany 89, 91, 92

For Product Safety Concerns and Information please contact our EU representative GPSR@taylorandfrancis.com
Taylor & Francis Verlag GmbH, Kaufingerstraße 24, 80331 München, Germany

www.ingramcontent.com/pod-product-compliance
Lightning Source LLC
Chambersburg PA
CBHW051756230426
43670CB00012B/2308